WALKING THE EDGES

Living in the Presence of God

DAVID ADAM

Illustrations by
Monica Capoferri

First published in Great Britain in 2003 by
Society for Promoting Christian Knowledge
Holy Trinity Church
Marylebone Road
London NW1 4DU

British Library Cataloguing-in-Publication Data
A catalogue record for this book is available from the
British Library

ISBN 0-281-05219-0

3 5 7 9 10 8 6 4

Typeset by WestKey Ltd, Falmouth, Cornwall
Printed in Great Britain by Bookmarque Ltd, Croydon, Surrey

Happy is the man who fails to stifle his vision
Teilhard de Chardin, *Hymn of the Universe*

Contents

Introduction

I was high up on the moor, sitting with my back to a dry-stone wall facing heather and bracken. On the other side of this wall was a beautiful green field full of sheep. As I ate my picnic, I began to think what made one side of this wall different to the other side. It was a person with some vision. Sometime in the past a farmer looked at the land and decided that, with hard work, he could change the land so that it was better for his flock. This then made me think of all the people I have known who have reached beyond what seemed to be the limit and extended their vision, their life, or the way they deal with the world around them. From experience I know it is not so much money but vision that limits our resources: we do not reach out because we believe that we have come to the edge of our capabilities. Too often people give up when they are on the edge of a breakthrough, or they choose security and comfort rather than risk adventurous living. We must learn to walk the edges of our experiences if we are to journey into God. As we are living and moving beings we cannot stand still for long: we will either reach forward and grow or stultify and start losing what we have had. This applies to individuals and their talents as well as to communities and churches. To live life to the full we have to reach out to the beyond, we have to seek to extend ourselves.

One of my favourite descriptions of heaven comes from County Kerry in Ireland. A woman was asked, 'Where do you think heaven is?' She replied, 'Heaven is about one foot six inches above the height of a man.' She was in no doubt that heaven was not far away but very near indeed. If you would only stretch yourself you could reach out and touch the borders of heaven, with a bit of effort you should be able to enter into it. Heaven is there, close at hand, and is waiting for us to become aware of its presence. There is no real boundary between heaven and earth, they are one: it is only our own blindness that prevents us entering into the kingdom. The reaching out for the other, the new, the strange, the different, can open us to the great Other who is God and who comes to us each moment of our lives. If we are afraid of the other, afraid to venture, if we seek security, safety and the status quo we are in danger of shutting God out. People who seek safety usually create a comfortable God in their own image. Faith helps us to cross borders and to walk into the unknown. Faith gives us the courage to enter new territories and to discover that all of life is a journey and an adventure. It was with these thoughts in mind I decided to look at a few people who had shown the closeness of the presence and become aware that the kingdom is at hand, people who knew that God was always with them and always ready to help them.

Because boundaries and borders have always had a fascination for me, I love to stand where the sea meets the land or to stand on a mountain peak.

Crossing from one country to another has its own excitement. I believe that many of the Celtic saints chose to live on borders, on boundaries between kingdoms; for on the edge of boundaries there is always the challenge to look beyond where you are, to look beyond what is in front of you and into the unknown. Boundary stones have also fascinated me, especially when some seem to mark boundaries between worlds. When I lived on the North Yorkshire Moors, I lived on the 'wrong' side of the wall, the place, according to Bede, fit for 'wild beasts or men who lived like wild beasts'. It was on the edge of this area that Cedd chose to build his monastery in what is now the village of Lastingham:

> Cedd chose a site for the monastery among some high and remote hills, which seemed more suitable for the dens of robbers and haunts of wild beasts than for human habitation. His purpose in this was to fulfil the prophecy of Isaiah [35.7]: 'in the haunts where dragons once dwelt shall be pastures, with reeds and rushes' and he wished the fruit of good works to spring up where formerly lived only wild beasts, or men who lived like the beasts.
>
> (Bede, *A History of the English Church and People*, Book 3, ch. 23, Sherley-Price, 1955, p. 177)

Cedd and his brother Chad no doubt made inroads to the area where I once lived and through their vision and activity changed it forever. The high moors are dotted with standing stones and crosses, most of them are at high points where you can see for miles. They might declare the boundary of a monastic area, but they also tell of another kingdom that is never far away from any of us. If we are unaware of the kingdom of God it is possibly because we have set our own boundary that we are afraid to cross. To hear the lives of such saints is to be encouraged to look beyond, to discover the God who is ever close at hand.

Now I live on the edge of England and Scotland, on the small island of Lindisfarne, where the tidal borders of the island are forever changing. Tourists come to the island in their thousands, sometimes thousands in one day, then the tide starts to close again and they leave. The island inhabitants move from hyperactivity into a time of quiet and peace, and it is as necessary to let the silence come around you as it is to let the pilgrims mill around you. We are lucky on Lindisfarne to have this natural rhythm: most people have to create this rhythm in their busy lives.

St Aidan came here to live a life of quiet adoration and then of activity, like the rhythm of the tides. On the island he would spend much time in silence and prayer, though there was teaching to do and many people to see to. When he left the island, he had to carry the silence in his heart in his many encounters with individuals and scattered communities. He lived under large open skies and beside the mighty sea; he would speak of a kingdom unseen, yet ever near. From the island his monks moved out to awaken a nation to the love and the presence of God and to tell that the kingdom of heaven is at hand.

Bede says of Aidan, 'His life is in marked contrast to the apathy of our own times, for all who accompanied him, whether monks or lay-folk, were required to meditate, that is, either to read the scriptures or to learn the Psalms' (Bede, *History*, Book 3, ch. 5, Sherley-Price, 1955, p. 145).

Wherever Aidan went he knew that God was with him and that God's love would not fail him. It was the message of the God of love he brought to a nation divided by war. People who had built barriers through fear and hatred began to lower the barriers in the name of Christ their Saviour. Aidan believed that Christ came not only to save people, but to break down the barriers that divide them. Aidan did not take God to people, but expected to meet God in the people he encountered. As an expression of this I wrote this poem on Lindisfarne:

> Within each piece of creation,
> within each person,
> the hidden God waits
> to surprise us with his glory.
>
> Within each moment of time,
> within each day and hour,
> the hidden God approaches us
> calling our name to make us his own.
>
> Within each human heart,
> within our innermost being,
> the hidden God touches us,
> to awaken us and to reveal his love.
>
> Everything, everyone is within God,
> all space, all time and every person.
> The hidden God asks us to open
> our eyes and our hearts to his presence.

For sixteen years Aidan taught lapsed Christians and non-Christians this wonderful message. Aidan sought to bring a people who were oppressed or oppressing to the glorious liberty of the children of God. Through Aidan a divided emerging nation would find a unity through Jesus Christ.

When Aidan died a young sixteen-year-old was looking after sheep in the Lammermuir Hills to the northwest of Holy Island. It was 31 August 651 and it was dark. Cuthbert was awake and very alert for he was protecting the flock; he had to be on the lookout for any strange thing and otherness about him. Suddenly he saw a vision in the night sky. Angels were coming down to the earth and then ascending. On their return journey they were taking 'a soul of exceeding brightness' to God. It was only the next day that Cuthbert discovered Aidan had died: the great Other, who is God, had broken into Cuthbert's life to change it forever. Pray that you never have such a vision, for life can never be the same again. The vision caused Cuthbert to 'subject himself to the grace of spiritual discipline and of earning everlasting life and happiness amid God's mighty men', which is Bede's way of saying he offered himself for the monastic life. But before this he said to his companions, who no doubt had slept through the time of the vision:

Alas, wretches that we are, who are given up to sleep and sloth and are not worthy to behold those servants of Christ who are ever watchful. For I myself, though I was watching in prayer for but a short part of the night, have nevertheless seen the wonders of God. The gate of heaven was opened and the spirit of a certain saint was conducted thither with an angelic retinue; and while we dwell in utter darkness, he now, blessed for ever, beholds the glory of the heavenly abode and Christ its King.

(Colgrave, 1985, p. 167)

If you live on borderlands, you need to keep alert and awake. There is always something going on at the edges, the otherness of life and the strange is always waiting to break into your life. For those who are alert and awake life will soon become an adventure. There is always more to see and to experience, for we are always on the borders of new worlds. The world is willing to offer to us wonder upon wonder if our senses are not dulled. To increase this sensitivity we need to be able to move out from the complexity of much of modern life to a simplicity of life that leaves room for things to happen. This simplicity will demand of us an abstinence from anything that would hinder our progress. It will compel us to find places where we can be alone, and yet not alone, for our God is with us. Simplicity, silence and solitude, which are often found in the remoteness of borders, will help to empty us so that there is room in our lives for God. In Hosea God says through the prophet, 'I will lead you into solitude and there I shall speak to your heart' (2.14). It is not necessary to travel to the edges of society to find stillness and peace: absence of noise or people is not necessarily peace. Silence is possible for all of us wherever we are in our minds and hearts. To achieve inner silence we will need to consciously depart from sound and into silence: we will have to create times of solitude as we travel to work or stand waiting for a train, when we can shut out the noise about us and enter into the stillness within. In the solitude of your own heart you can journey to meet God. Learn the great truth of the saying, 'Be still, and know that I am God' (Psalm 46.10). In the stillness and solitude of your own heart you can journey inwards to meet the God who is waiting there for you to come to him. Stillness allows us to cross into new territory and walk along new borders.

Jesus was often on the borderlands. Jesus sought out desert places and lonely places where he had space to be with the Father without being disturbed. He goes away by himself to pray. He is seen on the seashore and on the mountaintop. Throughout his life Jesus comes to and crosses borders. In the story of the madman of Gadara, Jesus is on the edge of life and death in a storm, on the edge of the lake, on the edge of another country, on the edge of reason, on the edge of violence, and here his powers are revealed. He is found on the fringes of society with publicans and sinners, with women of doubtful repute and with tax collectors. Jesus invited his disciples to the desert places after they returned from their mission, 'Come away by yourselves to a lonely place, and rest a while' (Mark 6.30–31). The people who did not want him to disturb them forced Jesus out of their presence: Jesus is edged out of the synagogue, out of the Temple, out of the city. He becomes more and more marginalized until he is edged out of life and into death: the cross itself shows that Jesus did not seek security or safety. Jesus will appear again from the edge of the grave, once again to be seen on the seashore and on the edge of a larger and more wonderful world.

We need to recognize the boundary places in our lives and our ability to enter into new worlds of experience. So many boundaries are of human fabrication which say, 'this far and no further', when in reality we can go on. We need to awaken to the reality that the world is far larger than our narrow vision. One of our leading feminists, has said, 'Most creatures are born blind and after a few days or weeks are able to see, most men, however, remain blind all their lives.' It is sad to think that many people, due to their own inability to see, miss what the poet Francis Thompson calls 'the many-splendoured thing'. Quite often when people say, 'I do not believe', they really mean they are unwilling to move from their blinkered position. They do not want to be stretched or to commit themselves to anything that would lead them out from where they are. Faith does not come without effort on our part, faith asks us to move out of our limiting security. God will call but we must open our ears. God will present himself to us, but we must open our eyes. God will offer us his love, but we must open our hearts. There is not much chance of having a healthy faith if we do not react to what is before us. There is as much chance of having a healthy faith without effort as there is of having a garden of roses without feeding the plants and pruning them. If we leave the garden to nature it will grow weeds: life as well as roses can revert to briars. Effort is necessary and this book is about people who were awakened, made the effort and so reached out beyond the frontier to the 'other' and the great 'Other' that was ever waiting to be known.

If we want to understand the doctrine we have to be willing to live the life: if we want to understand the way of heroes we have to be willing to live heroically, there is no half measure. If you do not enter fully into the life of faith, you will not be aware of what the written word is about. Secure theories can be learnt by anyone; true faith involves us fully and leads us to frontiers. God is ever on the edges of mystery and the unknown. Jean-Pierre de Caussade writes about Jacob's dream:

> 'Truly', said Jacob, 'God is in this place and I knew it not'. You are looking for God, dear soul, and he is everywhere ... he remains with you and you look for him! Oh, you are looking for your idea of God, while you possess his substance ... you are off chasing your sublime ideas ... God disguises himself to raise the soul to pure faith and to teach it to find him under all sorts of appearances; for once it has learned God's secret that he may well disguise himself, it simply says: He is there behind the wall, he is looking through the lattice, he is looking through the window.
>
> (De Caussade, 1933)

Jacob is my favourite story of awakening in the Bible (Genesis 28.10–22). There is no doubt that Jacob is a bit of a cheat. Twice he cheated his brother, once out of his birthright and then out of the blessing of heritage from his father Isaac. Jacob was not an ideal person. Jacob left his homeland for Haran. As the sun was setting he camped for the night. In his sleep he had a dream and he saw the angels of God descending and ascending a ladder that reached from heaven to earth. God speaks to Jacob and promises that he will not desert him. 'Then Jacob awoke from his sleep and said, "Truly the LORD is in this place and I never knew it". He was afraid and said, "How awe inspiring is this place and I never knew it. This is nothing less than the house of God and the gate of heaven." ' To remember this event, Jacob set up a standing stone and calls the place, 'The house of God'. Jacob's awakening was not just from a night's sleep but from a life with his eyes closed. Jacob moved into a new awareness of which he had not known before. In discovering a holy place, a house of God, he discovered that he did not leave his God at home but that God journeyed with him. Knowing the presence in one place meant that he learnt that God was with him wherever he went. Bethel was truly a place of awakening. I discovered that many of the standing stones on the Yorkshire Moors were set up about the same time that Jacob raised the stone at Bethel.

We must ask ourselves whether we have awoken out of sleep or are our eyes still closed? Have we awoken to the fact that our God is with us and will never leave us, that the ground on which we walk is holy ground? This book is to teach us that heaven and earth are not separate but are one, for us to learn that 'in him we live and move and have our being'. In *Le Milieu Divin* Teilhard de Chardin says,

> we have only had to go a little beyond the frontier of sensible appearances in order to see the divine welling up and showing through ... By means of all created things, without exception, the divine assails us, penetrates us and moulds us. We imagine it as distant and inaccessible, whereas in fact we live steeped in its burning layers.
>
> (Teilhard de Chardin, 1964, p. 112)

This is God's earth and he is to be found within it: we need to set out with joy to cross the boundaries that have prevented us from seeing and knowing the presence and power of our God. God is with us and waiting for us to come to him; his kingdom is near and waiting for us to enjoy it. Though it may not be a burning bush, or storm, earthquake and fire, our God still approaches us through his creation, our hidden God waits for us to find him in the ordinary. One day we will awaken and discover that nothing on this earth is ordinary, for all things have the extraordinary ability of revealing our God to us. We will then know, with Julian of Norwich, 'We are more in heaven than on earth.'

Here is a thought from an English folk poem by an unknown author that expresses the same thoughts, if we will take it seriously:

> This is the Key of the Kingdom;
> In that Kingdom is a city;
> In that city is a town;
> In that town is a street;
> In that street there winds a lane;
> In that lane there is a yard;
> In that yard there is a house;
> In that house there waits a room;
> In that room an empty bed;
> And on that bed a basket –
> A Basket of Sweet Flowers;
> Of flowers, of Flowers;
> A Basket of Sweet Flowers.
>
> Flowers in a Basket;
> Basket on the bed;
> Bed in the chamber;
> Chamber in the house;
> House in the weedy yard;
> Yard in the winding lane;
> Lane in the broad street;
> Street in the high town;
> Town in the city;
> City in the Kingdom –

This is the Key of the Kingdom,
Of the Kingdom this is the Key.

(De La Mare, 1928, p. 3)

The Scriptures proclaim that Jesus has broken down the walls that divide us, and that the kingdom is here and to be entered into: seek to make that a reality in your daily life. Discover that the great Other, who is God, is ever present, 'and in him we live and move and have our being'.

Exercises

1 Read Genesis 28.10–22. Seek to imagine yourself in the place of Jacob. Have you awoken out of sleep? Can you say 'Surely the LORD is in this place'? Do you live in awareness of this reality? Acknowledge God's presence in your life, in your home, at your work, wherever you are and say 'The Lord is here. His Spirit is with us.'

2 Think over these words from 'The Kingdom of God' by Francis Thompson:

O world invisible, we view thee,
O world intangible, we touch thee,
O world unknowable, we know thee,
Inapprehensible, we clutch thee!

Does the fish soar to find the ocean,
The eagle plunge to find the air –
That we ask of the stars in motion
If they have rumour of thee there?

Not where the wheeling systems darken,
And our benumbed conceiving soars! –

The drift of pinions, would we hearken,
Beats at our own clay shuttered doors.

The angels keep their ancient places;–
Turn but a stone, and start a wing!
'Tis ye, 'tis your estranged faces,
That miss the many-splendoured thing.

3 Pray:

Lord, open our eyes that we sleep not in death.
Awaken us to your glory
Dispel the darkness of night
Open our eyes to your presence
Open our ears to your call
Open our hearts to your love
Awaken us to your glory.

4   Be still and know. Small silences, little stillness,
secret solitudes – God makes them sacred. In
silence, stillness and solitude let the soul seek for
God.

Silence is the solitude of the heart
Silence is the soul's healer
Silence is the speech of lovers
Silence is the saint's shelter
Silence is the strength of the faithful
Silence is the search for God who comes
    to meet you.

Martin, Soldier for Christ

The Borders of England and Scotland are my homeland and have always held a great fascination for me.
Every hill and river seems to have a historical story or
a folk-tale. I was fortunate to have a father who was
interested in story and so learnt much as I travelled
around with him in his wagon. One road we often
travelled was the 'Military Road' that runs for the
most part alongside Hadrian's Wall. Hadrian's Wall is
surely the most imposing of all Roman fortifications
in Britain. The Wall, which was sometimes called the
Picts' Wall, is 73 miles long with milecastles and forts
from the Tyne to the Solway, almost from coast to
coast. Along its length it had 320 turrets. It has been
suggested that it must have had about 10,000 men to
patrol the length of the Wall.

For me the Wall was a place to dream about and
hope to find long-lost treasures, a place to stretch
myself. I looked at where King Arthur was said to be
sleeping and could be roused if he was needed. I visited
many Roman forts and saw traces of early Christianity. I loved walking along stretches of the Wall and
getting caught up in the romance of Border skir-
mishes. Often I would stop at the place with the

wonderful name of Twice Brewed and make for the Wall, then walk up Peel Crags by the stone staircase towards Cuddy's Crag and on to Housesteads. The views from along this part of the wall are breathtaking and so is the Christian history of the area. Cuddy's Crag is named after St Cuthbert; no doubt he travelled this way on his way from Lindisfarne to Carlisle. To the west is Haltwhistle, where the tradition says Eden Green is a corruption of Aidan's Green and that St Aidan preached there. Further west from Cuddy's Crag is the fort of Birdoswald, the largest fort on the Wall and perhaps the birthplace of St Patrick; we will come back to this later. Beyond Birdoswald is Brampton, where there is a small fort built by a Roman auxiliary unit in about AD 125 to control the area whilst the Wall was being built. In this fort are the remains of a late fourth-century to fifth-century church dedicated to Martin of Tours. The remains of the church are surrounded by an almost circular cemetery. There used to be an ancient oak tree in this area called Martin's oak. Nearby is Ninewells, Ninian's Well, named after one of the great saints of the fifth century. To the south is the Roman Camp of Vindolanda and here in 1998 was discovered the remains of a fifth-century church constructed in the courtyard of the villa belonging to the fort's commander. The villa was used from 220 until the Romans withdrew in 410. It is thought that the church was built about the time of the Roman army leaving. The worshippers probably numbered no more than 12–15 families and were mainly descendants of the troops who had occupied the fort. If St Patrick was born in this area, his grandfather may well have ministered to some of these Christian communities. Further east along the Wall is a village with the name of Wall. It is near here that Oswald had his vision of St Columba visiting him and then raised a cross to remind his men that God was with them. Cuthbert often travelled the Wall to be at the western edge of his pastoral oversight. We hear of him in the Carlisle area more than once and often at great physical cost to himself.

These saints who are mentioned along the Wall are the ones I would like to look at in this book, especially their vision and contribution to extending the frontiers of the faith. I would like to look at Martin, Ninian, Patrick, Oswald and Cuthbert. These men worked when earthly kingdoms were in turmoil, when life was tenuous; they saw beyond to the kingdom of God, to peace and to life everlasting. Such visionaries have a message for our times which are so often not at peace and offer a hope for us all.

The Roman army along the wall was drawn from all parts of the Empire. From contemporary records known as *Notitia Dignitatum* we have a list of the army and civilians working along the Wall. The men came from Italy, from North Africa. There were Asturians from Spain, Frisii from the Frisian Islands, Tungarians and Batavians from Teutonic lands, Dacians from Romania, Dalmatians from Yugoslavia. There were Syrian archers, but the ones that caught my attention were the Pannonians from what is now Hungary. I was interested because I knew that Martin's parents came from Pannonia.

Martin was born at Sabaria in Pannonia in 316, but was brought up at Ticinum, which is in Italy.

His parents were, according to the judgement of the world, of no mean rank, but were heathens. His father was at first simply a soldier within the ranks, but afterwards was raised to be a military tribune. The Roman legions of Pannonia were renowned as a training ground for elite officers, and from their ranks a number of emperors had emerged. The Emperor Decius had been born in Pannonia of Italian parents, and the emperors Claudius II, Aurelian, Probus, Diocletian and Constantine were all of Illyrian peasant families. Martin's father belonged to this elite corps: beginning in the ranks he was promoted to military tribune, which was as high as was normally possible if you did not come from an aristocratic family. I wondered what would have happened if Martin's father had been posted to the Wall instead of Gaul.

As a youth Martin must have learnt of the persecution of Christians by the Emperor Diocletian. When he was about four years old, 40 soldiers from around Cappadocia refused to sacrifice to the gods of the Empire, saying 'We are Christians.' The governor tried to bribe the soldiers to concede, but they replied, 'All that you offer us is of a world that is perishing, we despise that world. We look for our reward in heaven, and we only fear hell.' The weather was well below zero. The soldiers were stripped and marched onto a frozen lake. A sentry was put in place on the shore and they were there to stay for the night. The sentry had a warm fire to protect him. Throughout the night the soldiers on the lake sang, 'Forty martyrs went out to fight, let forty martyrs be given the crown.' One of the 40 soldiers weakened and went to warm himself at the fire. The sentry, moved by the courage of his fellow soldiers, stripped off his cloak and ran down to replace the man who had weakened. In the morning all had perished and their dead bodies were taken away to be burned. Their heroic deed would not be forgotten. There were many similar stories of martyrs and their witness that Martin must have heard, stories of men and women who saw clearly another kingdom, and the presence of a saving God. As ever, the blood of the martyrs was the seed for the growth of the church. In a world looking for comfort and safety, here were men and women not afraid to risk and to die, to live boldly in the temporal because they were aware of the eternal.

By the time Martin was old enough to seek a martyr's crown the Diocletian persecutions were over; in fact he was only about nine when they ended. The other event Martin would have heard about was from a world that was excited about the dawning of a new era, a Christian era. This was the story of a Roman soldier who became the Emperor. A young 18-year-old Roman soldier, Constantine, had seen a vision in the sky as the sun was setting: in the heavens he saw a great cross and heard a voice saying, 'In this sign conquer.' From that moment Constantine had gone on to conquer all his enemies and all that opposed him. It was as if nothing could stop him. Many were convinced he had 'God on his side'. When Constantine became the new Caesar, he not only stopped the persecution of Christians, he went out of his way to restore their churches and to help them grow. In fact he favoured the Christians so much that it was said he wanted everyone to become a believer in the Christ. It was said that Constantine's mother,

Helen, had found the true cross of Christ outside Jerusalem. It was an exciting time for the Church, which was growing and becoming attractive, at the very time the Empire was beginning to struggle. For the first time, much of the Empire was being drawn to the Church, even if not yet for the right reasons.

The church in Ticinum, with its newly found approval, attracted the young Martin. The secret symbol of the Christians, the Chi-Rho, being the first two letters of 'Christ' in Greek, was beginning to appear on the sacred standards of his father's legion and throughout the whole of the Roman army. The church was becoming a respectable and a safe place to go to. Among their increasing numbers came the young Martin. Martin's biographer Sulpitius Severus wrote:

> When he was ten years old, he took himself, against the wishes of his parents to the Church, and begged that he might become a catechumen. Soon afterwards, becoming in a wonderful manner devoted to God, when he was twelve, he desired to enter the life of a hermit: and would have followed up that desire with the necessary vows, had not his as yet too youthful age prevented.

There can be little doubt that here was a church that was attractive, and lively: a church that was open, accepting and understanding. From this early contact Martin obviously got a glimpse of a heroic way of service and living. The church was obviously a place of mystery and of story. Many of the stories were about the heroic lives of saints and hermits. These tales caught the imagination of the child. He wanted to live a heroic life; already he wanted to go into the wilderness and wrestle with demons. Here in the church, which was also the bishop's house, the bishop would have personally signed him with the cross as the beginning of his dedication to Christ, and then the bishop would pray for his time of preparation as he laid his hands on the child's head. From this time until Martin was almost 15 Sulpitius wrote that Martin was 'always engaged in matters pertaining to the ministries of the church, already meditating in his boyish years what he afterwards, as a professed servant of Christ, fulfilled'.

So often if a young person can be inspired in these early years of their life they will never lose the vision that was their joy and their challenge. We need to make sure our churches are attractive and challenging to all who come. They need to be places that help people to see beyond and to extend themselves.

Living in a small council house, I can remember being inspired by the stillness and the size of St Michael's church in Alnwick. I was able to go from working in dark damp surroundings underground in a coal-mine to assist at an altar of golden angels. Yet I was never allowed to enter the small sanctuary of this side altar until I had recited Psalm 43. I soon knew this off by heart, and I mean heart, for I did not learn it by rote for my head and memory. I learnt it in worship, in awe and adoration of God. There was something quite wonderful about leaving the coal-mine behind and saying:

> O send out thy light and thy truth, that they
> may lead me: and bring me unto thy holy hill,
> and to thy dwelling.

> And that I may go unto the altar of God, even unto
> the God of my joy and gladness ...
>> (Psalm 43.3–4, Book of Common Prayer).

I learnt my unworthiness before God and confessed it before him, but also through God's grace and goodness I could enter his sanctuary with joy. Even now, half a century later, I do not enter a sanctuary without a pause and an act of reverence. The old priest at Alnwick, who was a Latin scholar, managed to help me to understand my early strivings in the faith: the same way at Ticinum the church captured Martin. My father found it strange that I should put myself out for weekday worship and at what he called 'ungodly hours', especially as I was on shift work and had to make a great effort to be there. At this stage I was learning that discipleship needed discipline as well as a teacher. I was also slowly learning that if you find a holy place, the presence of God goes with you and all places are holy.

The story of the old priest handing on the faith to the young is as old as the Jewish faith. In 1 Samuel 3.1–10, we learn of the child Samuel and the old priest, Eli. One who was 'ancient', with his vision failing and the light of the sanctuary going out, was given the child Samuel to look after. Eli's own sons did not want to follow in their father's footsteps. The old man was tired and wanted to sleep; he did not want his way of life to be disturbed. The child Samuel was the last sort of gift the old man wanted: the energy and enthusiasm of the child would disrupt his days and disturb his sleep. In the silence of Shiloh the old man slept and the child Samuel was alert for anyone who called.

Samuel was attentive in case Eli wanted him in the night, his ears tuned to the stillness. Into this solitude and stillness came the voice of God, calling 'Samuel, Samuel.' Three times Samuel heard the call and three times he disturbed the old man's slumber. At first Eli tried to get Samuel to go back to sleep. Then he who was old and nearly blind saw clearly. Eli saw that it was the LORD calling the boy; in this child the word of God would be heard. 'It is the LORD calling you. If it happens again, and it will, say "Speak, LORD, for your servant is listening."' In this way, in the holy place, Samuel was guided and given an understanding of life and its mysteries. The same event happens over and over again in the history of the Church. The Church thought to be old and lacking in vision is the guardian of the faith; through wisdom and tradition the Church helps each generation to understand who they are and the world about them. An age that ignores the wisdom of the past is in danger of floundering on a stormy sea. To not accept the guidance and experience of others is to be foolish and irresponsible.

The guardians of the faith are greatly privileged in having received the faith and it is their responsibility to hand it on, that in turn the recipients may be enriched and enrich it. New people help the light of faith to burn more brightly. Very often the Church is privileged to guide and nurture someone who is destined to do great things for the world and for God. We do not know much about the church at Ticinum or its priest, but we do know it set Martin on his journey to become a shining light in the Church.

We are left in no doubt that Martin was growing in the faith. Probably the Church as well as Martin himself had plans for his future. As Martin was given a vision of heroic living he was encouraged to live heroically. Hearing of the desert fathers, Martin wanted to become an athlete for God; he wanted to be a hermit and wrestle against the powers of evil. No doubt he was told to pray, to learn psalms and to wait, as he was only a child. There would be plenty of opportunities to wrestle with and fight against the powers of evil later in his life.

His soldier father had other ideas. There were battles and other campaigns to be won. Barbarian forces were gathering at the edges of the Empire. Constantine had posted a notice in every garrison demanding that sons of veteran soldiers should be constrained by force if necessary to join the army. When the Danube frontier was at risk in 331 the age of recruitment of soldiers' families was brought down to 16. Martin's father saw that recruitment was an opportunity to get this young man away from his fancies and into the army. His father told the recruiting officer that Martin should join the ranks but warned him of his stubborn nature. When the officer came to the house he came unannounced and prepared. To Martin's horror, the officer arrived with a set of manacles to take him off to serve in the army. Martin had been hoping to leave home soon for a desert place and become a hermit; instead he was driven off for 25 years' service in the army. No doubt his parents were delighted, believing that the army would make a man of him. Serving in the army was not a barren period in Martin's life but a time for learning discipline, obedience and orderliness. Much of what Martin introduced into his way of monastic life at a later period comes from his learning in the army. This time is not a lost time: the Roman soldier was in training to become a soldier of Christ and many of the disciplines are the same.

So often when we look back on what seemed to be against what we had planned we discover that it was a point of growth and learning. God does not work only within the confines of the Church or of our own ideas: it is often when we are forced to do other than we planned that the great Other works through us. I do not believe in vocation as much as vocations. God does not call us once but again and again and again. Vocation is being open to the situation we are in and listening to what God is saying within it. If our vocation is thwarted at one level it does not mean that God not longer calls us: God calls us wherever we are, we are called to keep ourselves aware.

Serving as a soldier demands submission to superiors, simplicity of life, singularity of purpose, separation from others. All of these disciplines would enrich Martin and give him a pattern to live by for the rest of his life. Through commanding officers, drill exercises, strict orders and punishments for disobedience, soldiers learnt obedience. Without obedience the army would not survive. Martin would learn that such obedience, in time, brought its own freedom: just as Christians would talk of Christ 'whose service is perfect freedom'.

Soldiers had to travel lightly so they were relatively poor, at least until they retired. A soldier was not to be hampered by carrying around too many possessions; most things would be held in common. Soldiers shared the same camp and food. Food was often of the simplest sort, with meat a rare luxury. Quite often it was only one meal a day and that would be of something made of wheat or some other grain.

Because soldiers were often on the move and had to leave quickly, celibacy was the ideal. For centuries it had been the rule that all serving men were unattached. Only in the third century with more settled garrisons did it become acceptable for a soldier to marry; but celibacy was still looked upon as the ideal.

Martin was learning through the army the basics of obedience, poverty and chastity, plus frugal eating, if not fasting. The freedom that came from these ideals Martin would build up into the monastic life of his first community when the opportunity came. In later life when Martin managed to become a hermit his renown brought him many disciples and he was hardly ever alone. The time in the army prepared him for building up an army for Christ.

After his initial training, as a tribune's son Martin would be given many privileges. He would have the right to serve in his father's corps and be immediately promoted to the rank of under-officer. He would have the right to a double ration of food, to have a servant and to own his own horse. More importantly, such a position gave him more freedom and space than the rank and file, space he would use to continue to prepare for his baptism. He was not the only Christian in the army; that the faith was spreading over the Empire was often due to presence of Christians in the army.

From the beginning of his army career Martin was determined to live the life of a dedicated Christian. He spent time helping any who were in trouble, using his military pay to help the needy and keeping only what was necessary for his daily sustenance. The beggars that collected around the church at Amiens where he was stationed found a good friend and helper. Martin treated his own servant as an equal and used to take turns in cleaning the servant's boots and waiting upon him. Already, in many ways, he was acting more like a monk than a soldier.

There are two events in Martin's life as a soldier that would be told throughout the Empire. The first happened on a severely cold night in a winter that was proving fatal to many, especially the poor. Martin met a beggar at the city gate of Amiens. At the time, the 20-year-old Martin had no money, only the military clothes he stood up in and his weapons. The poor man was almost without clothing and calling for help. All who passed him by ignored him. There were too many beggars to take notice of them all. Martin stopped and looked upon the man with compassion. Yet what should he do? He had already given his money away and had nothing left of use except the cloak he was wearing. Martin quickly decided to share his cloak with the beggar. He drew his sword and, dividing the cloak into two equal parts, he gave half to the beggar. As Martin walked away with half a cloak around him, some of those who saw it laughed at his foolishness. It is said that others had a twinge of conscience for they had more than Martin and had done nothing. The same night, when Martin lay down to sleep, he had a dream. Martin saw Christ wearing half a cloak. As Martin watched he was told that this was the cloak with which he had clothed the poor man. Then he heard in a loud voice Christ speaking to the angels of heaven and saying, 'Look what Martin, who is still a catechumen, has clothed me with this day.'

There are moments in all our lives when something happens to open our eyes or deepen our normal sense of perception, moments that if we allow them will change our lives forever. Sometimes momentary experiences will carry us for years if not for the rest of our lives. Such experiences are hard to put into words because if a person has not had a similar experience they will not really know what we are talking about. Martin was sure that he had met the Christ in a beggar. He would not be the first or the last to encounter the living Lord. Saul met the Christ on the road to Damascus. He saw nothing but a blinding light yet he heard the voice that said, 'I am Jesus, whom you are persecuting' (Acts 9.5). The incarnation, though unique in Christ is not a past event but an eternal reality, and we are able to encounter the Christ in human form. The Incarnate Lord is present in this world and wants us to meet up with him. The Christ is not confined to books or to history. He is the living Lord and we will meet him on our travels often in the most unexpected of disguises.

There many experiences similar to that of Martin, probably the two best known being those of St Christopher and St Francis. Christopher was a Christ seeker and wanted to meet up with the Christ personally. After much searching, Christopher was persuaded that if he would but wait on others he would meet the Christ. This is still a good way of encounter. Christopher took on the work of looking after travellers across a dangerous ford, caring for their safety. To the ford came a child needing to be carried across the swollen waters. Christopher used all his strength and ability as he got into deeper and deeper water. He carried the child shoulder high. In simple response to the child's cry for help Christopher gave himself fully. On reaching the other shore, Christopher put the child down and proceeded to dry himself. During this time the child disappeared and Christopher was convinced that he had carried the Christ child. Even if the child had just gone off home, Christopher had met the Christ. Even if the child had another name, Christopher knew that it was Christ he had dealt with at the ford.

Francis of Assisi was used to caring for others and sought to express God's love for all of creation. This was not too difficult when he was dealing with birds or ordinary, needy folk. We can all love the lovely but find it hard to accept the ugly and the unlovable; this often takes a great act of will and discipline as well as a great heart. Such a confrontation asks that you see beyond the obvious to the extra-ordinary depth that is there. It was much harder for Francis when he was confronted with a leper needing his love. Suddenly he was faced with one who was scorned and rejected by society, one who had apparently no beauty. The look of the leper repulsed him and made him feel sick. Francis knew he had to master his feelings, he could not ignore this man. He took the leper into his embrace and enfolded him in brotherly love. As he held the leper he knew he embraced the Christ and that the Christ embraced him. That poor man's face was the face of Christ. The great Other had come to Francis in the other poor man before him.

Each of these saints had discovered in depth the sacrament of the incarnation, of the Word which became 'flesh and dwelt among us' (John 1.14). They learnt the reality of the words of Jesus, 'as you did it to one of the least of these my brethren, you did it to me' (Matthew 25.40). They each had the ability to see Christ in the other and at the same time to be Christ to the other. Such an experience cannot leave us unmoved, for such an experience has the ability to change our lives forever. It was after visiting someone in hospital and then feeding a tramp that called at the vicarage that I wrote:

> You are the caller,
> You are the poor,
> You are the stranger
> At my door.
>
> You are the wanderer
> The unfed,
> You are the homeless
> With no bed.
>
> You are the man
> Driven insane,
> You are the child
> Crying in pain.
>
> You are the other
> Who comes to me.
> If I open to another
> You are born in me.

(Adam, 1985, p. 34)

This is not some sentimental experience, it is life transforming. When you meet Christ in the other it will affect the way you deal with anyone: forever the words, 'as you did it to one of the least of these' will influence all your dealings. Vision, if it is not just fantasy, is always life changing. The privilege of seeing Christ in the other demands that we treat every individual with respect, we cannot pick and choose where we want the Christ to be met. We may have this vision about one individual but it will then affect our dealings with everyone. After his vision of Christ wearing half of his cloak, Martin completed his final preparations for baptism from the bishop of Amiens.

Martin continued to serve in the army and other fellow Christians did the same. He would spend the first half of his life within the confines of the army. Martin at the age of 40 was detailed to serve under the Emperor Julian. The same Julian was beginning to reintroduce into the army old pagan ways. Martin had come to the end of his term of office and was about to leave the ranks, planning once more to become a hermit. Julian's army was under threat by the barbarians. At this same time Martin was offered a long-service award by Julian, but Martin replied to Caesar:

> I have served you as a soldier: allow me now to become a soldier of God: let the man who will serve you receive your gift. I am a soldier of Christ and it is not lawful for me to fight.

This was an uncomfortable encounter for Julian and he was furious and declared that Martin was acting not so much as a Christian but as a coward. In response Martin declared,

> If you think this is cowardice and not faith, I will take my stand unarmed in the forefront of the battle tomorrow. I will be protected not by shield or helmet but by the name

of the Lord Jesus, and the sign of the cross. So, I will safely penetrate the ranks of the enemy.

Julian ordered Martin to be put into prison until the morning when he would be put in the front line of the troops without weapons or protection. Fortunately for Martin, the next day the barbarians sent ambassadors to plead for peace and surrender. It was rumoured by many that Martin had brought about this peace by his actions. For the Celtic peoples this story meant more, for it was the function of their Druids to stand between opposing armies and to establish peace. No doubt Martin had spent the time in prison praying to God as his protector. It was William Temple who said, 'When I pray coincidences happen, and when I do not pray they do not happen.' Whatever we make of the event, which was talked of throughout the Empire, Julian decided it was not wise to have such a man leading his troops and so released Martin from the army as he requested.

There are times when it is uncomfortable if not dangerous to make a stand, but when God calls we need to answer. If we ignore God's voice we become deaf to his call: if we refuse to act upon what we see we become more short-sighted and vision becomes blurred. If we have never been uncomfortable with our faith it is likely that we have not allowed it to stretch us.

When Martin was released from the army, he set off towards Poitiers, towards its first bishop, Hilary, and towards his hope of becoming a hermit. When welcomed by Hilary, Martin felt that this was where he was meant to be. With Hilary he would learn of the joy of being a Christian, and how they would sing joyfully to the Lord. However, Hilary was about to go into exile in Phrygia for speaking out against the Emperor Constantius. Hilary must have thought of Martin as a true 'God send' in this time of need. With Martin, Hilary had gained a man who was used to making decisions and being in control. Martin was made a deacon and so became part of the small group of deacons that assisted Hilary in maintaining worship, caring for the faithful in Poitiers. The deacons lived in the same house as Hilary and shared a common life given to prayer, fasting, Scripture reading and meditation. Here Martin would be schooled in the understanding of the Trinity and warned against the Arian heresy, which was so popular at the time. He learnt that God was not a single person but an inter-reaction of three persons in the one Godhead. Hilary would also make sure all his deacons understood that (contrary to the Arian view) Christ was truly human and truly divine. Soon Martin was appointed as an exorcist with special care for the mentally ill and the handicapped within the city and surrounding district. Martin was now a soldier of Christ and took seriously his battle against evil. Once again this was not quite what Martin had hoped for; his desire to become a hermit was balanced with obedience and his care for others.

Within a year of joining Hilary, Martin dreamed that he should go and visit his parents who were over 1,000 miles away in Sabaria. Hilary encouraged him to go on this journey, as he was about to go into exile. Whilst travelling Martin said he met Satan in a human form. The devil asked him where he was going. Martin replied that he would go wherever the Lord called him. In reply to this the devil said, 'Wherever you go or whatever you do the devil will resist you.' In answer Martin repeated a line from the Psalms: 'The Lord is my helper; I will not fear what man can do to me.' As he said this, the devil vanished immediately out of his sight. As a soldier of Christ, Martin had already learnt that he could not fight just in his own strength, he needed the armour of God. This event shows how Martin knew his Psalms and also was well aware that he would face many struggles in his desire to serve his God. Martin did not belittle evil, or think that if he had won one round of the battle he had won the war: he was well aware that the more he tried to serve God the more the evil of the world would oppose him.

I had a friend who was an old soldier. Life was never easy for him: if you asked him how he was, he would reply, 'Battling on.' In the Christian life if we are not fighting against evil it is most likely that we have compromised in our way of living. Personal temptations are always with us if we are truly alive. I risk saying to the person that is never tempted, 'Get yourself a life!' Temptation is often the option to take the easy way out or to avoid any conflict, it is the flight to comfort and security. Martin saw himself as a soldier and part of the 'Church Militant here on earth'. We are called to share with Christ in the world's redemption, and to fail is to fail our Lord.

In 361, when Martin heard that Hilary had returned from exile, Martin returned to Poitiers. On his return, Martin was given a country villa belonging to Hilary, 13 km from Poitiers. The villa had been destroyed by an invading army and never repaired; in the hillside were natural caves, a clear running stream and enough land for cultivation. Martin could be self-supporting: all he would need was a mattock, a spade and some corn. Here he was to spend the happiest ten years of his life. There would be a rhythm of prayer, study and manual labour. Around Martin would grow a community. The place would become named Liguge, 'the place of little cells'. Here he would begin the way of community living he would continue when he became the bishop of Tours. It was during these years Martin became known for living the gospel he preached, often in poverty and always trusting in God. His fame began to spread throughout the land. What would inspire people as much as his words was his lifestyle: his actions proclaimed the faith he taught.

In 371 the bishop of Tours died and a deputation from the town came to seek Martin to be their bishop. This visit must have reminded Martin of when he first lost his freedom and was taken away by the recruiting officer from his home. Martin would try to live up to people's expectations and be the sort of person they wanted him to be, but if he had succeeded we would have never known of this saint. It was no use trying to fulfil the role others set when he knew God's agenda was wider and different. There was a danger that in becoming a bishop he would get caught up in the politics and administration that has so often beset the bishop's office.

It would appear this group would not accept any refusal. Though not all wanted this poor brother, the popular opinion won the day. The people carried Martin off by force away from his beloved Liguge. At this time what shocked many of the more respectable citizens was Martin's haircut: it was the sort of haircut that was to become the distinctive style of Celtic monks, shaved off at the front from ear to ear, leaving the brow and forehead bare. Some believed that this was the hairstyle of Celtic warriors, others saw it as the awkwardness of a rustic.

Only for the first few months did Martin live in the bishop's house in Tours. Martin longed for a simpler way of life than he found in the bishop's house and wanted to return to his hermitage. He did not want to spend his time administering properties and looking after important visitors to the city, he wanted to spend more time in prayer. The bishop's house was a busy place, more like offices than a church, and it was hard to devote the proper time to prayer. Some even said that Martin lost some of his holiness by allowing himself to be made a bishop. There was a danger that much administration would take over what he saw as his real work. One day without warning he moved from the church premises and out of the city altogether. He went to the caves that dotted the south bank of the Loire. The area looked very like Ligugé but on a much grander scale. It was here that the first bishop of Tours had lived during the times of persecution 150 years before. Martin built himself a wooden hut at the foot of one of the highest of the cliffs. This way of life was in great contrast to the way the bishops were now used to living. The Church had come into a time of security and relative wealth, it had become urbanized and bishops were expected to be important people living in cities. Martin was choosing a way of poverty and insecurity, a way of vulnerability. Many thought it not fitting for a bishop to live in poverty, but others were attracted to Martin and to his heroic way of living. For many the mainstream Christian Church had ceased to be a place where they were challenged to live heroically and they needed to be stretched more in their faith.

I was looking for adventure when I was a teenager. I wanted to be stretched and to grow in body, mind and spirit. Having worked in the coal-mine, I was a little suspicious of the comfortable life of a theological college. Then I heard of Kelham. A priest told me it was like the commando course of the Church of England. He told of rising at 6.00 a.m., of compulsory cold showers, of having few if any possessions, and of much silence. The whole idea frightened and yet attracted me. 'They turn out men ready for action, able to do battle with the problems around them. You will learn to serve God by scrubbing floors, shovelling coal and playing football.' It all seemed a far cry from what I thought a theological college would be like but I wanted to go there and have never regretted it. Life needs to be an adventure or something within us dies. We are not called to talk of adventures past like some ageing colonel having drinks at the club, we are called to be God's soldiers to battle against evil and win the world for Christ.

Many adventurous Christians sought out Martin at what became known as Marmoutier. They lived like the sand martins in the caves that dotted the cliff side. Here came about 2,000 men seeking to dedicate their lives to prayer and the service of God. These men held everything in common. If a rich man joined, for a while they might look as if they were prospering, but as they gave to the poor and bought slaves to set them free, they often ended up living in poverty themselves. The days were divided up by the saying of regular prayers and the singing of hymns; no doubt some of these were hymns written by Hilary. Martin as their leader wore the simple rough serge of a slave. As many of the brethren wore the same garb it was not easy to notice the great leader of this community. The more time Martin sought to spend in quiet the more he seemed to be attracting others to join him. In Martin they saw a man who was content with God, a man who witnessed to his faith by the way he enjoyed the presence of God. People flocked to Marmoutier for spiritual guidance, or just to be near him and to follow his example. The soldier of Christ was building an army for God. It was now that Martin's early training came into its full use: the army discipline, obedience, ability to travel lightly, to go a day without food, all became part of the common pattern of living. It was also saying that here in the ranks of the army was a good way of learning to serve Christ. If a person does not learn discipline, they will not learn to be a disciple. Martin knew that regular food was important to his men but he knew that they and the world had a greater hunger. When we learn to control our many appetites we discover what we really need, and what truly satisfies our hunger.

Martin still went out in mission seeking to win the pagans for Christ. Such missions were conducted like a military campaign with Martin's troop of monks coming out of their camp and into the territory of the enemy. He knew that it was not wise to enter the enemy camp alone or without proper preparation. He believed that though they were a small army they had great power through their God. The following is an account of one such battle for the soldier of Christ as related by Sulpitius Severus in his *Life of Martin*:

In a certain town after destroying a very ancient temple, Martin desired also to fell a pine tree which stood close to the site of the pagan sanctuary. But the priest of the place and all the heathen population obstinately set themselves to oppose him. These men who by the grace of God, had silently allowed the destruction of their temple, were now determined that the tree should not be felled.

All in vain did Martin forcibly represent to them that there was nothing worthy of veneration in a mere tree, that they should not worship it, but rather the great God whose minister he was, and that this tree which had been dedicated to a devil should be cast down.

At length one of the heathen, bolder than the rest, exclaimed: 'If thou hadst conquered in the name and in the power of this God whom thou pretendest to adore, we, ourselves, will fell this tree, but only on the condition that thou place thyself beneath it, so that in its fall it will crush thee. If thy God is ever with thee, as thou declarest, thou will run no risk.'

Bold and confident in the Lord, Martin at once agreed to the proposal.

This strange bargain caused a vast concourse of pagans to assembly. They were resigned to the loss of their sacred tree if only its fall might cause the destruction of the enemy of their faith.

The great pine tree had grown to one side and it seemed certain that in falling it would crash in the direction towards which it leant. Martin, therefore, was bound with and placed in a certain spot indicated by the peasants and where they were convinced the tree must fall. And then the pagans began to fell the tree – joyfully, eagerly, did they go to work in full view of a crowd of persons who, all amazed watched from afar.

Soon the pine tree shook and trembled and it seemed that the Saint must surely be crushed to death.

The monks, standing afar off, grew pale, terrified at the imminent peril. They had lost all hope, all courage, and were convinced that Martin must die.

He however, strong in the Lord waits fearless, undisturbed, and as the crashing noise made by the falling tree reverberates through the air, he calmly raises his hand and makes the Sign of the Cross. The tree seems to be caught backwards by some unseen power and it falls in quite the opposite direction to which it inclined, so that the peasants, who were gathered in what had appeared to be a safe place, have a narrow escape from being crushed to death.

At once, a great shout rises up to Heaven – the pagans are amazed and confounded by the miracle and all the monks weep for joy. All acclaim the name of Christ and indeed on that day salvation was vouchsafed to the whole district, for in all that great crowd of heathen there was hardly one who did not implore the laying on of hands in order to believe in the Lord Jesus and abandon the errors of paganism.

And truly before Martin's day, very few, hardly any of these regions had professed Christ, but now the Holy Name became so well known, thanks to the miracles and the examples of Martin, that the whole district is full of churches and monasteries. Martin's practice being, wherever he destroyed heathen sanctuaries to replace them immediately with churches and monasteries.

From the final sentence of this episode, we learn of the wisdom of Martin: he understood that 'a cleansed house would not remain empty'. If the temple was not replaced by something better the pagans would soon revert to their old ways. In this world of growing Christianity and its onward mission, Martin and his followers were taking over the pagan sites and building their churches and monasteries in their place.

Obviously, the use of the timber and stone from such sites made their task the easier, but more importantly the place to which the people had been used to coming was still there for their use. The law of the Empire demanded that if temples fell into disuse they should be handed over to the Empire for secular purposes, such as theatres or markets. In the Eastern part of the Empire this did happen. Martin's influence and that of his followers claimed such places for Christ. These claimed temples became outposts of the faith manned by small groups of soldiers of Christ. Like the soldiers on Hadrian's Wall, the little bands of monks guarded the outposts of Christianity and kept the enemy at bay. There is no doubt that Martin knew his Scriptures, and would be familiar with the story of the haunted house:

> When the unclean spirit has gone out of a man, he passes through waterless places seeking rest, but he finds none. Then he says, 'I will return to my house from which I came.' And when he comes he finds it empty, swept, and put in order. Then he goes and brings with him seven other spirits more evil than himself, and they enter and dwell there; and the last state of that man becomes worse than the first.
>
> (Matthew 12.43–45)

This experience is true of gardens, houses, people, in fact all of nature for nature abhors a vacuum. People and the land will need to be filled with something or

the weeds take over. Flowers do not flourish unless
they are planted and neither does goodness. I like, at
the beginning of teaching meditation, to ask people to
empty their minds: in no time they are confronted with
bad thoughts or memories so I keep this period short!
It shows that if we just empty our minds they will soon
be filled with rubbish; we must choose what we put
into them. Evil can be driven out but it will return even
stronger unless you replace it with something else.

In a sense the mind is like some great record. Everything you see, do and experience is taped, kept somewhere in your memory. At times we can choose what
we want to remember, at other times it seems the
memory works on random selection. It follows that
the quality of the material you put on the tape is
the quality of the material you will have for playback,
and remember that you are not always in charge of
selection. Here is a lovely poem from a Celtic monk
with the title 'On the flightiness of thought':

> Shame on my thoughts, how they stray from me!
> I fear great danger from it on the day of eternal
> Doom.
>
> During the psalms they wander on a path that is not
> right:
> They fash, they fret, they misbehave before the eyes
> of the great God.
>
> Through eager crowds, through companies of wanton
> women,
> Through woods, through cities – swifter they are than
> the wind.

Now through paths of loveliness, anon of riotous
shame!
Without ferry or ever missing a step they go across
every sea:
Swiftly they leap in one bound from earth to heaven.

They run a race of folly anear and afar:
After a course of giddiness they rerun to their own
home.

Though one tries to bind them or put shackles on
their feet,
They are neither constant nor mindful to take a spell
of rest.

Neither sword-edge nor crack of whip will keep them
down strongly:
As slippery as an eel's tail they glide out of my grasp.

Neither lock nor firm-vaulted dungeon nor any fetter
on earth,
Stronghold nor sea, nor bleak fastness restrains them
from their course.

O beloved truly chaste Christ to whom every eye is
clear,
May the grace of the seven-fold Spirit come to keep
them, to check them!

Rule this heart of mine, O dread God of the elements,
That Thou mayst be my love, that I may do Thy will.

That I may reach Christ with chosen companions,
that we may be together!
They are neither fickle nor inconstant – not as *I* am.

(Meyer, 1928, pp. 35–6)

If we want to drive out evil and to keep God's peace in our minds and hearts, we need to heed the words in the letter to the Philippians 4.8: 'Whatever is true, whatever is honourable, whatever is just, whatever is pure, whatever is lovely, whatever is gracious, if there is any excellence or anything worthy of praise, think about these things.' The more good you put into the system, the more is likely to come out at times of random selection. If you fill your life with rubbish it will produce rubbish. If we do not care what we see and hear we have already given in to evil. Let us never belittle the battle or we will lose what goodness we can achieve.

The outposts that were near enough to Marmoutier were visited regularly by their leader. Martin, like some military general reviewing his troops, would see to discipline and campaigns for action. He would see that people were being looked after pastorally and that they were given the opportunity to grow in the faith. He knew that if souls were to be won for Christ the battle against evil would be relentless. It was necessary to check that his men were performing their duties in winning souls for Christ. It was necessary to see that lives were being filled with the love and peace of God, for it would not happen without effort. Martin would then return to his own cell to spend time in prayer and meditation. God was his priority and he fought against the powers of evil within his own life. If you do not wrestle with your own inner battle God does not get the opportunity to overcome what is taking over his place.

It has been suggested that Ninian and Patrick visited Martin, and that Columba and Columbanus visited his tomb. We shall never know who came to

Marmoutier, but we do know the enduring influence of Martin. Even when the Roman Empire had collapsed and the Dark Ages arrived, pilgrims flocked to the tomb of Martin at Marmoutier. There was a church dedicated to St Martin at Canterbury well before the arrival of Augustine, there is a St Martin's cross on Iona, and an early church dedicated to Martin near Hadrian's Wall. His biographer Sulpitius Severus reminds us well of Martin's renown:

> The Ethiopian knows his fame; the Indian too has heard of it as have also the dwellers in Persia and Parthia. Armenia has not been left in ignorance, nor has the region beyond the Bosphorus; and surely, if there be dwellers in the Fortunate Isles and the Arctic regions, they, too, must have heard of the fame of Martin.

Exercises

1 Thinking about Martin and the beggar, here is an Irish poem about hospitality for you to reflect upon:

> O King of the stars!
> Whether my house be dark or bright,
> Never shall it be closed to anyone,
> Lest Christ close his House against me.
>
> If there be a guest in your house
> And you conceal aught from him
> 'Tis not the guest that will be without it,
> But Jesus Mary's Son.
>
> (Meyer, 1928, p. 100)

2 Read Matthew 25.31–46. Then read these verses from the ancient poem 'The Lyke Wake Dirge'. It

is believed that this poem was often recited at the wake before a funeral.

> If ever thou gavest hosen and shoon
> Every night and all,
> Sit thee doon and put them on;
> And Christ receive thy soul.
>
> If hosen and shoon thou gavest nane
> Every night and all,
> The whins shall prick thee to the bare bane;
> And Christ receive thy soul.
>
> If ever thou gavest meat and drink
> Every night and all,
> The fire will never make thee shrink;
> And Christ receive thy soul.
>
> If meat and drink thou gavest nane
> Every night and all,
> The fire will burn thee to the bare bane;
> And Christ receive thy soul.

3 In Martin's desire to be a hermit, he never neglected the call of the Church community. Think over these words by Dietrich Bonhoeffer from his book *Life Together*:

> Let him who cannot be alone beware of community ... Let him who is not in community beware of being alone ... One who wants fellowship without solitude plunges into the void of words and feelings, and one who seeks solitude without fellowship perishes in the abyss of vanity, self-infatuation and despair.
> (Bonhoeffer, 1952 pp. 77–8)

4 A good way to approach God is with someone in your heart: a good way to approach someone is

with God in your heart. Listen to God on behalf of others: listen to others on behalf of God. Make sure you give your undivided attention to each one in their own right. Try to meet people and approach God this way for at least a week.

5 Offer yourself to God in the words of this hymn:

> Make me a captive, Lord,
> And then I shall be free;
> Force me to render up my sword,
> And I shall conqueror be.
> I sink in life's alarms
> When by myself I stand;
> Imprison me within thine arms,
> And strong shall be my hand.
>
> My power is faint and low
> Till I have learned to serve;
> It wants the needed fire to glow,
> It wants the breeze to nerve:
> It cannot freely move,
> Till thou hast wrought its chain;
> Enslave it with thy matchless love,
> And deathless it shall reign.
>
> My will is not my own
> Till thou hast made it thine;
> If it would reach a monarch's throne
> It must a crown resign;
> It only stands unbent,
> Amid the clashing strife,
> When on thy bosom it has leant
> And found in thee its life.
>
> (George Matheson, 1842–1906)

Ninian, a Bright Star

From the edge of the Roman Empire and looking towards the world's edge we hear of Ninian. According to tradition, Ninian was a tall man and of good physical build, and his father, the chief of a tribe, wanted him to become a soldier. Ninian from an early age wanted to learn more of Christ and to serve him; this sounds very like Martin of Tours. It would be good if we knew how Ninian received the faith and whether Christianity had reached Whithorn before Ninian's own mission. There are certainly signs along the border of England and Scotland of Christian activity in the late fifth century. In the Ettrick Valley, near to some fifth-century Christian burials, someone has carved a praying figure with bare feet and cropped hair, wearing a knee-length garment marked with the cross. There are also memorials in the Yarrow Valley, at Peebles. The place name Eccles comes from the Greek word for church. This is later than Ninian, but maybe the area was Christian well before this time. Whatever the truth might be, Ninian certainly received his faith from someone unknown: before Ninian's mission there were obviously some Christians at the work of mission and outreach in his area. From a cultured people who honoured warriors, suddenly appears a man who wants to be a soldier for Christ and who was inspired by Martin from the beginning of his call. Writing in the eighth century, a monk from Whithorn said of Ninian:

> God omnipotent, who had scattered shining lights upon the world, gave many bright stars to his people in Britain. Brilliant among these was Ninian. He was outstanding in strength derived from heaven, in miracles, in eloquence and reliance on the gift of God. People came together in vast crowds and opened their hearts to believe in Christ and to follow his teaching.

How could such a great man be almost forgotten, and not numbered among the great saints of the land? There were probably early records of the deeds of Ninian, but they have all disappeared due to the raids of the Anglo-Saxons and the Vikings. Here is a saint working well before Augustine of Canterbury, and setting up a monastery, in what is now Scotland, well before Columba of Iona. With people like Ninian we get a glimpse of the lives of early Christians in Britain and of their link with Europe. We hear little about him because he was from the 'wrong side of the wall': he was not orthodox enough to be claimed by the Roman Church, and the rise in importance of Iona as a founding church eclipsed the stories of the outreach and mission of Ninian.

The earliest account we have of Ninian is in the writings of the Venerable Bede, and that is about 300 years after Ninian. Bede writes:

The southern Picts, who live on this side of the mountains, are said to have abandoned the errors of idolatry ... and had accepted the true Faith through the preaching of Bishop Ninian, a most reverend and holy man of British race, who had been regularly instructed in the mysteries of the Christian Faith in Rome. Ninian's own Episcopal see, named after saint Martin, and famous for its stately church, is now used by the English, and it is here that his body and those of the saints lie at rest. The place belongs to the province of Bernicia, and is commonly known as *Candida Casa*, the White House, because he built the church of stone, which was unusual among the Britons.

(*History of the English Church and People*,
Book 3, Ch. 4, Sherley-Price, 1955, p. 143)

As a historian, Bede seeks to be precise in his use of words to describe nations and peoples, and he is careful to distinguish between the Britons and the Picts. Ninian is described as a Briton who worked among the Southern Picts. Bede was writing from Northumbria whose northern frontier was the Forth estuary. It is most likely that Bede counted all that lived south of the Clyde–Forth line as the Britons including northern England and that those to the north of the line were the Picts. The Britons were thought to have been Christian and the Picts pagan. Ninian's base was in the land of the Britons and his mission seen to be among the Picts beyond the Clyde and Forth.

Did Ninian really go to Rome, and was he made bishop whilst he was there? We shall never know. This may be an attempt to make Ninian more orthodox, and show that he was a proper bishop in the style of the Roman Church. A little like the stone at Whithorn that says 'The place of Peter the Apostle', and so claims the place for orthodoxy. Yet there is no reason why Ninian did not travel to Rome and spend time there in learning before being consecrated as a bishop to return to the 'end of the world'. In the same way there is no reason why Ninian should not have spent a good deal of time at Marmoutier with St Martin. One of the things we seem to forget is the amazing distances the early saints were willing and able to travel throughout the Christian world. Some have suggested that Ninian did not visit Martin but was inspired by the *Life of Martin* written by Sulpitius Severus. There is no doubt that the stories concerning Martin were the talk of the Empire and the Christian world. We all need to know the stories of the heroes of our faith, if we are truly to grow in the faith. A Church or a nation without stories is impoverished.

I was attracted to the Church by stories of local saints who were super-heroes, men and women who could stand against evil and conquer nations. In junior school I heard of Aidan, Oswald, Cuthbert, Caedmon, Bede and their great deeds. This was not like hearing of past campaigns of an army but of what could be done by people of faith. What I learnt then in a school atmosphere I have tried to emulate in my life. We will not understand the deeds of the saints unless we try to live like them.

Ninian's buildings were known as *Candida Casa*, usually translated as the White House, and so giving the name to Whithorn, Anglo-Saxon Hwit Aern, meaning White House. The word *casa* implies a poor sort of dwelling of the kind erected by monks in the wilderness. Bede uses the word *casa* to describe the monastic infirmary at Whitby where Caedmon the poet died.

Casa was used in Gaul to describe the most basic of monastic buildings. Often the mortar of such building was a coarse creamy white, which tended to make it stand out in the landscape. It is possible that *Candida Casa* meant the 'shining', or the 'radiant' house and this was more about the glory and the holiness of the house rather than its colour. As ever, it is not what a church looks like so much as what it stands for and what it does. Churches by their nature are meant to reveal the radiance and the glory of God.

When my call to the priesthood was in its earliest days I cycled high onto the moors and discovered an ancient church. There was no one to be seen anywhere, the only sounds outside were the sheep and the birds. Inside the church there was a great simplicity, a stillness that suggested here was a holy place used for over 1,000 years. The flowers in vases were fresh, telling me the church was still looked after and used by the small moorland community. The sun shone through the stained glass windows casting patterns on the paving. What really caught my eye were the words painted in green on the east wall above the window, 'Come into His presence with thanksgiving'. How could I do otherwise? I learnt from that moment that one of the best approaches to God is thanksgiving and the opportunity for stillness and solitude. I do not know any member of that congregation, but I know their church has a radiance that is expressed through their love and care.

The twelfth-century monk from Rievaulx in North Yorkshire suggested in his *Life of Ninian* that St Martin died whilst *Candida Casa* was being built: this was the year 397 and we have here the first firm date for Christianity in what is now Scotland. Aelred tells of how Ninian brought men across from Gaul to build the church. This again is possible, but it is more likely that the men Ninian brought were needed to build up the church as a community. More than masons, Ninian needed a group of men who would build up the Christian presence and further the growth of the Church in the Solway area and beyond. This is a little like St Francis, who thought he was called to build up a fallen down church building when in reality his call was to build up the Church community, a church of people not of stones. The Church was there before the building. In fact it is likely that they worshipped in the open long before the building was ready. It is a pity we talk of 'going to church'; we are the Church and you cannot go to what you are. The building is where we meet as the Church and is meant to express our belief in God's presence everywhere.

Aelred tells of Ninian consecrating bishops as well as ordaining priests and deacons. If this is correct, then, like the bishops of the Celtic Church that would grow from such places as Whithorn, Ninian did not feel the need to have three bishops present to consecrate other bishops, as was required by the Church of Rome.

In the *Life* by Aelred we get glimpses of genuine old stories that must have been handed down by word of mouth in and around Whithorn. Aelred also had use of an earlier Life, which he calls 'barbarous in its content'. This early Life may have been based on a Celtic Life now lost. From the old stories we get a glimpse of some of the real struggles that Ninian was caught up in and some of his attitudes to life.

Aelred writes that shortly after founding *Candida Casa*, Ninian came into conflict with a local chief called Tudwal, who is described as 'the king of the Manu'. It has been suggested that the Manu was the Gododdin Manu who were in control of the area around the Firth of Forth and it would seem that Ninian went to this area. However, it is more than likely that Manu is in this case the Isle of Man.

Tudwal, who was described as being 'as cruel as he was ungodly', was opposed to Ninian and some of his followers working in his territory. Tudwal objected to 'flocks from many nations' coming to Manu: he did not like this foreign interference and so expelled the members of Ninian's community. It sounds as if from the beginning Ninian's community came from many nations: could some of these be the 'church builders' from Gaul? Soon after his opposition, Tudwal was struck blind and his crops failed; he personally believed it was because of his treatment of Ninian. At Tudwal's invitation Ninian returned, the land then prospered and Tudwal's sight returned. From this we get a glimpse of the mission of the community from *Candida Casa* and that it was also faced with local opposition. It might be that the story was told to show how Tudwal was blind spiritually until he accepted the true faith, and only then did his land prosper. Being aware of their Scriptures, these early saints were in no doubt that 'Where there is no vision, the people perish' (Proverbs 29.18, Authorized Version). Short-sighted acts cause as much danger in our world now as they have ever done. It is still true that 'in the country of the blind the one who sees is counted as mad'. The land, communities and individuals only prosper when there is some vision and purpose. Unless we have an idea of whom we are and what we are called to do, no amount of activity or distraction will satisfy us.

Ninian's community obviously grew and prospered. We hear of Ninian going to visit his flocks and his shepherds in their huts to give them his blessing. For this purpose he had all his flocks gathered in one place. Because night was coming on, he enclosed the flocks within a circle he drew on the ground. The circle was to protect the flocks from any evil; it was a symbol of the protecting power and love of God. This is very much a Celtic action: the circle is known as a Caim and it shows that God and his love are always round about us. When the Celtic Christians felt they were endangered in any way they drew the Caim about them in the way a person would draw a cloak about them to keep out the cold. Sometimes, a Caim was made by a person using the index finger of their right hand and turning sunwise in a circle, to remind them that they lived in the presence and power of God. On other occasions the Caim was a defence work of earth or stone put up around their community. Very often the Caim defence was not high enough to keep out invaders, but it was seen as a special defence symbolizing God's protection. Such a defence was in no way magic, but an expression of the abiding presence and power of God. The Caim was an acting out that God is with us and cares for us. If we can carry this awareness with us it will certainly transform our lives and our attitude.

The Caim around a community also demanded a reaction from those who entered within it, for it expressed a desire to recreate Eden or that God's king-dom come now on earth as in heaven. There was a desire by all who lived within such a circle to live according to the will of God and to his glory; anyone who did not heed this could not be allowed to live within the area. The making of the circle demanded standards by which all within would live and it asked for an awareness of God, his power and his will. The Caim around a community suggested within is hospitality not hostility, is peace not the sword. With-in the circle was an opportunity to live life as God wanted it to be. I can remember an old priest saying to me, 'If you pray "your kingdom come", let it begin in your own house, tidy your room, clear your desk, redecorate and do all to the glory of God. Let it come in your mind, let hostility be turned to hospitality, let there be peace within. If you want God's kingdom to come start with yourself.' I believe that communities surrounded by a Caim were attempting to do just that, to herald in God's kingdom on earth. Once you have your community living that way then you can reach out to others.

There are many Caim prayers from the Outer Hebrides. One of my favourites is the Smooring of the Fire, which is said as the peat fire is dampened down, smoored, for the night. The embers are evenly spread out in a circle, which is then divided into three equal parts with a small boss in the middle. A peat is now laid in each section. The first peat is laid in the name of the God of Life, the second in the name of the God of Peace, the third in the name of the God of Grace. At the same time this prayer is said:

The sacred Three
To save,
To shield,
To surround
The hearth,
The house,
The household,
This eve,
This night,
Oh! This eve,
This night,
And every night,
Each single night.
     Amen

                (Carmichael, 1983, p. 235)

There is also a beautiful Caim for the protection of
a person, which was often said before they went on a
journey:

The compassing of God be on thee,
The compassing of the God of life.

The compassing of Christ be on thee,
The compassing of the Christ of love.

The compassing of the Spirit be on thee,
The compassing of the Spirit of Grace.

The compassing of the Three be on thee,
The compassing of the Three preserve thee,
The compassing of the Three preserve thee.

                (Carmichael, 1976, p. 105)

Ninian would have said such a protection prayer over
his flock as he left them for the night. This did not

mean he would leave them exposed to any danger
without attention. It did mean as they were dedicated
to God, no one should harm them. After his prayers
Ninian went out to see to his flock to find that thieves
had invaded the circle thinking the flock unprotected.
The leader of the thieves lay dead and the rest were in
great terror, unable to escape. Ninian prayed that the
dead man's life might be restored, and he recovered
from death. After telling them all about the evil of
thieving they were let go free. Though the story may be
hard for us to accept, it tells us of the way these early
Christians thought; they were sure that sin brings
about death and God's forgiveness is life-restoring.
There was a firm belief that whoever breaks God's
law brings trouble upon themselves. It is not so much
that God punishes them as that they suffer from a
self-inflicted wound. The early Christians of this land
would have agreed with the thoughts in the poem
'Hound of Heaven' by Francis Thompson:

All things betray thee, who betrayest me.

And

Naught shelters thee, who will not shelter me.

Too often in our modern society we blame God or
others for wounds and pain that are in reality
self-inflicted. Our attitude to the world brings about a
response from the world. We are learning that if we do
not respect the environment we will bring trouble
upon ourselves. Disrespect for the air we breathe or
the waters of the earth threatens to bring disaster
to our planet. Unless we change our attitude towards

our use of fossil fuels we are endangering future generations.

Another story that gives us many insights into the way of life at Whithorn is the theft of Ninian's bachall, or staff. Many of the stories of Celtic saints tell of this staff, which sounds like a staff of authority but was not a bishop's crozier. Aelred writes:

> Meanwhile many, both nobles and men of middle rank, intrusted their sons to the blessed Pontiff to be trained in sacred learning. He indoctrinated these by his knowledge, he formed them by his example, curbing by any salutary discipline the vices to which their age was prone, and persuasively inculcating the virtues by which they might live soberly, righteously and piously. Once upon a time one of these young men committed a fault, which could not escape the saint, and because it was not right that discipline should be withheld from the offender, the rods, the severest torments of boys, were made ready. The lad in terror fled, but not being ignorant of the power of the holy man, was careful to carry away with him the staff on which he used to lean, thinking he had procured the best comfort for the journey, if he took with him anything that belonged to the saint. Flying therefore from the face of the man, he sought diligently for a ship, which might transport him to Scotia. It is the custom in the neighbourhood to frame of twigs a certain vessel in the form of a cup, of such a size that it can contain three men sitting close together. By stretching an ox-hide over it, they render it not only buoyant, but actually impenetrable by water. Possibly vessels of immense size were built in the same way. The young man stumbled on one of these lying at the shore, but not covered in leather, into which he had incautiously entered, by Divine providence, I know not whether for its natural lightness (for on a

slight touch these float far out into the waves), the ship was carried out to sea. As the sea poured in the unhappy sailor stood in ignorance what he should do, whither he should turn, what course he should pursue. If he abandoned the vessel his life is in danger: certain death awaited him if he continue. Then at length the unhappy boy, repenting his flight, beheld with pale countenance the waves ready to avenge the injury done to the father. At length coming to himself, and thinking that Ninian was present in his staff, he confessed his fault, as if in his presence, in a lamentable voice, besought pardon and prayed that by his most holy merits the divine aid might be vouchsafed to him. Then trusting in the known kindness as well as the power of the bishop, he stuck the staff in one of the holes, that posterity might not be ignorant of what Ninian could do even on the sea. At once, at the touch of the staff, the element trembled, and as if kept back by divine influence, ventured not to enter further by the open holes ... a wind rising from the easterly quarter impelled the vessel gently. The staff acting for a sail caught the wind; the staff as helm directed the vessel; the staff as anchor stayed it. The people standing on the western shore, and seeing a little vessel like a bird resting on the waters, neither propelled by sail, nor moved by oar, nor guided by helm, wondered what this miracle might mean.

In this story Aelred talks of the using of a coracle and wonders about bigger seaworthy boats such as the curragh. It is thought that Aelred would have no awareness of a coracle, as they were not used in his native Yorkshire. We catch a glimpse of the monastery trying to keep discipline among its young men, and this was not to spare the rod. If the idea of the monastic enclosure was to create a heaven on earth, or a new

Eden, it could not have its young men being disobedient or acting contrary to the will of God. Discipline was essential for the growth of a healthy community. We cannot learn to play the piano without accepting the disciplines of scales and much practice. We cannot learn to take part in a sport unless we accept the rules and train ourselves to achieve. We cannot grow in the Christian faith unless we willingly accept its disciplines and commit ourselves to doing God's will and seeking his glory.

Whatever the stories tell us, there is no doubt that for a good while *Candida Casa* flourished, men came for learning, priests were trained, and new outposts of mission and learning were set up. There was another early Christian settlement to the west of Whithorn on the next peninsula at Kirkmadrine. There are two tombstones at Kirkmadrine dating from about the end of the fifth century. One is dedicated to Viventius and Mavorious, 'the holy and outstandingly excellent bishops'. The other stone also describes a pair of monk bishops. It makes one wonder whether they were fulfilling the instruction of our Lord and going out to preach and teach in twos, as these stones tell of two such teams.

We know from the story of Tudwal that Ninian sent people to the Isle of Man. The area of Strathclyde shows many place names and legends linked with Ninian. A church at Brampton by the river Irthing has a chapel dedicated to St Martin. Here the well which belonged to the Roman fort now has the name of Ninewells (Ninian's well). At 'the Home of the Badger', Brougham near Penrith, in what was the Roman civil settlement is Brougham Ninekirks, which is Ninian's Church. At the other end of the kingdom of Strathclyde, just south of Stirling, is a place still bearing the name Saint Ninian. Tradition has it that Ninian consecrated a cemetery at Glasgow before the arrival of St Kentigern. There are many churches named after Ninian in Scotland and Northern England, but it cannot be safe to claim all of these as places that he visited. There is no doubt that Ninian reached beyond the Roman Empire and into the land of the Picts, to the Isle of Man, and at least his pupils reached across to Ireland, if he did not go himself. Finnian, who founded the monasteries of Moville in County Down and Dromin in Louth, received some of his education at *Candida Casa*. Finnian had among his pupils Columba, who would found many monasteries including Iona. The first teacher of Columbanus was Sinell, a disciple of Finnian who had learnt from Ninian, so we see how the gospel spreads out like a bright light enlightening one place after another.

Not far from Whithorn on the seashore is Glasserton, and the place of Ninian's hermitage. When you sit outside Ninian's cave on the shore at Glasserton, you can feel his desire for a place set apart, just like Martin at Marmoutier. No doubt when Ninian needed to meditate and spend time in quiet he would retreat to the cave. The view from the cave is itself inspiring: across the sea is the Isle of Man rising like a great rock, on the far horizon is Ireland, to the north is the Kingdom of Strathclyde and the Rhinns of Galloway. Ninian must have often sat on the shore and dreamed of conquering kingdoms for Christ. In the mainstream Church this was a time of retreat, as the Empire was retreating. If the Church reached out, it reached out in safety to people of a similar culture as

their own. Ninian was reaching out to the 'barbarians', to those who had not been conquered by Rome,
though Rome had certainly influenced them. The west
side of the country was by far the easiest way to be in
contact with the continent because of the Gulf Stream.
The North Sea was a barrier for any easy movement
north and south. All of this placed Ninian in a stra-
tegic position for outreach and mission.

The cave at Glasserton and *Candida Casa* point to a
rhythm of life that moved between activity and
outreach and then a return to stillness and solitude:
a balance between serving people and worshipping
God. It is popular to say that the Church exists for
mission; this only a half-truth for the Church exists to
worship God and to give glory to him. The hyper-
active Church is in danger of offering itself and a way
of being busy without reference to God: even some
study groups are in danger of talking more about
God than they ever talk to him. A Church certainly
exists more for mission than for the maintenance of
buildings and to keep the status quo, but a Church
must be seen to delight in God and to enjoy his
presence. For all its programmes the Church must
make sure there is room for stillness and awareness of
our God: activity must always be balanced by stillness
and rest. If we do not spend time receiving from God
we will soon have nothing to give out. Too often
people are sent out in 'mission' before they have had
time to know their God whom they are proclaiming;
we need to spend time getting to know God before we
ever go out. If we truly get to know our God we will
discover he is a sending God and it is his mission that
we are called to take part in.

Candida Casa as a place of learning spread its influence through its pupils. The pity is we know little of what Ninian taught or how he taught it. The following is by tradition associated with Ninian. Though most probably written later, it does express some of the ideas of an early monastic establishment:

Ninian's Catechism

Question	What is best in the world?
Answer	To do the will of our Maker.
Question	What is his will?
Answer	That we should live according to the laws of his creation.
Question	How do we know those laws?
Answer	By study – studying the Scriptures with devotion.
Question	What tool has our Maker provided for this study?
Answer	The intellect, which can probe every thing.
Question	And what is the fruit of study?
Answer	To perceive the eternal Word of God reflected in every plant and insect, every bird and animal, and every man and woman.

(Van de Weyer, 1990, p. 96)

Here we find a desire to discover the presence of God in all things, something that modern Christians seem to fear. Because of the fear of pantheism, many Christians seem to have banned God from his creation. A friend of mind who is a bishop says, 'I do not like saying, "The Lord is here" within a service.' This brought from me the response, 'If he is not here, then where is he?' The bishop, being a deep thinker, was instant in his reply, 'I do not want to give the impression that God is only in church.' So my final comment on the matter was, 'Well then, go around the supermarkets, the railway stations, the factories and declare "God is here" by your presence, your care, your self-giving.' We need to show God's presence by our actions rather than by mere words. From a time near that of Ninian, we get a wonderful declaration by Pelagius of the presence of God:

> Look at the animals roaming the forest: God's spirit dwells within them. Look at the birds flying across the sky: God's spirit dwells within them. Look at the tiny insects crawling upon the grass: God's spirit dwells within them. Look at the fish in the river and sea: God's spirit dwells within them. There is no creature on earth in whom God's spirit is absent. Travel across the ocean to the most distant land, and you will find God's spirit in all the creatures there. Climb up the highest mountain, and you will find God's spirit among the creatures who live at the summit. When God pronounced that his creation was good, it was not only that his hand had fashioned every creature; it was that his breath had brought every creature to life.
>
> Look too at the great trees of the forest; look at the wild flowers and the grass in the field; look even at your crops. God's spirit is present within all plants as well. The presence of God's spirit in all living beings is what makes them beautiful; and if we look with God's eyes nothing on the earth is ugly.

One of the great gifts from the Celtic Church to us is this emphasis on the presence of God at all times and in all things. There is no separation into sacred and secular, into body and soul, into heaven and earth. All are one in God. There is nothing outside of God or his love. It is only our blindness that prevents us from seeing the glory that is all about us. From a modern Celt, Teilhard de Chardin:

> God who made man that he might seek him – God whom we try to apprehend by the groping of our lives – that self same God is as pervasive and perceptible as the atmosphere in which we are bathed. He encompasses us on all sides, like the world itself. What prevents you then, from enfolding him in your arms? Only one thing: your inability to see him ... The true God, the Christian God, will under your gaze, invade the universe, ... He will penetrate it as a ray of light does a crystal ... God truly waits for us in things, unless indeed he advances to meet us.
>
> (Teilhard de Chardin, 1964, pp. 46–7)

Ninian's Catechism inspired me to write the following:

> Within each piece of creation,
> within each person,
> the hidden God waits
> to cause us to laugh and surprise us with his glory.
>
> Within each moment of time,
> within each day and each hour
> the hidden God approaches us
> to call our name and to give us his joy.
>
> Within each human heart,
> within our innermost being
> the hidden God touches us
> to awaken us to his love and his presence.
>
> Everything is within Him,
> Space and time,
> The human being and the heart.

God calls us to open our eyes
and our hearts to Him and his will.

I had learnt at college that all things could be done to the glory of God, and I learnt the hard way. I was told every task could be for God's glory and that meant it had to be done well. I was then told to go and clean the urinals and 'it means cleaning where no one sees around the bends. Know that whatever work you do it is for the forwarding or the hindrance of his kingdom.' Later I would read these words by Gerard Manley Hopkins about how to begin to give glory to God:

> Turn then, brethren, now and give God glory. You do say grace at meals and thank and praise God for your daily bread, so far so good, but thank and praise him now for everything. When a man is in God's grace and free from mortal sin, then everything he does, so long as there is no sin in it, gives God glory, and what does not give him glory has some, however little, sin in it. It is not only prayer that gives God glory but work. Smiting an anvil, sawing a beam, whitewashing a wall, driving horses, sweeping, scouring, everything gives God some glory if being in his grace you do it as your duty. To go to communion worthily gives God great glory, but to take food in thankfulness and temperance gives him glory too. To lift up the hands in prayer gives God glory, but a man with a dung fork in his hand, a woman with a sloppail, give him glory too. He is so great that all things give him glory if you mean they should. So then, my brethren live.
>
> (Gardner, 1953, p. 144)

I have taken this advice to heart and along with Ninian's Catechism I have found it a great guide to enjoying the world and having a glimpse of the glory of God.

Exercises

1 Think on these words:

> Apprehend God in all things, for God is in all things, every single creature is full of God and is a book about God. Every creature is a word of God. If I spent enough time with even the tiniest of creatures – even a caterpillar – I would never have to prepare a sermon. So full of God is every creature.
>
> (Meister Eckhart)

Peter of Damascus says:

> We must remember God at all times, in all places, in every occupation. If you are making something, you must call to mind the creator of all things; if you behold the light, do not forget him who gave it to you; if you see the heavens and the earth, the sea and all that is in them, glorify and marvel at their maker. When you put on your clothes, recall whose gift they are, and give thanks to him who in his providence takes thought for your life. In short, make every action an occasion for ascribing glory to God, and see you will be praying without ceasing: and in this way your souls will be always filled with rejoicing.
>
> (Quoted in Harries, 1983, p. x)

Do seek to 'apprehend God in all things, for God is in all things'. Let the word become flesh and dwell among us that we may behold his glory.

2 Do not forget, not only do you dwell in God, he dwells in you.

Affirm (for it is not a request but a reality):

> God be in my head
> And in my understanding.
> God be in my eyes

And in my looking.
God be in my mouth
And in my speaking.
God be in my heart
And in my thinking.
God be at my end
And at my departing.

(*Pynson's Horae*, 1514)

3 Practise the Caim.

Visualize yourself encircled by the love, the light, the peace of God.

Make a circle by using the index finger of your right hand, extending your arm and slowly turning clockwise until you have made a circle in which you are enclosed. Then say:

Circle me, O God,
Keep peace within
Trouble out.

Circle me, O God,
Keep love within
Hatred out.

Circle me, O God,
Keep light within
And darkness out.

Learn to rest in that love, that light, that peace. Know that God is with you, before you and behind you. God will protect you from your past and in the future. Let his presence give you light, love and peace.

Then, radiate the love and light and peace. Visualize other people surrounded by God and immersed in his presence. The people you pray for, see them surrounded by light, by the love of God, by his peace, and know that this is a reality if only we have eyes to see.

See the light, love and peace that God gives to you rippling out in waves in the way a stone makes waves when it is thrown into a pond. Reach out in prayer to others. Pray that they may know the reality that God is life and joy and peace.

4 You may like to end this session by using the prayer attributed to St Francis:

> Lord, make me a channel of your peace.
> Where there is hatred, let me sow love;
> Where there is injury, pardon;
> Where there is discord, union;
> Where there is doubt, faith;
> Where there is despair, hope;
> Where there is darkness, light;
> Where there is sadness, joy;
> For your mercy and your truth's sake. Amen.

Patrick, Pilgrim for the Love of God

Perhaps the best known of all the Celtic saints is Patrick. We are fortunate that he wrote about himself in the *Confession*, where we discover how Patrick was able to survive over what would seem to be insurmountable odds. Time and again life seemed to be against Patrick, but he survived and went from strength to strength. Patrick leaves us in no doubt that it was his trust in God that helped him to survive when others were at a loss. Due to his early misfortune, Patrick learnt to put his faith in the Almighty and ever-loving God:

> I, first a rustic, a fugitive and unlearned, indeed not knowing how to provide for the future ... Who aroused me, a fool, from the midst of those who appear to be wise, and skilled in the laws, and powerful in speech and in every matter? And me – who am detested by this world – He has inspired me beyond others (if indeed I be such), but on condition that with fear and reverence, and without complaining I should faithfully serve the nation – to which the love of Christ has transferred me, and given me

for my life – if I should be worthy – that in fine, I should serve them with humility and truth.

(*Confession*, §§ 12–13)

Patrick, aware of his own unworthiness but also aware of the power of God, sounds like St Paul: knowing himself to be a fool called to reveal the wisdom of God he echoes 1 Corinthians 1.27–9:

> God chose the foolish things of the world to shame the wise: God chose the weak things of the world to shame the strong. He chose the lowly things of the world and the despised things – and the things that are not – to nullify the things that are, so that no one may boast before him.

When I was called from the coal-face to offer myself to the priesthood, I was also greatly aware of my ignorance, not only of ordinary world knowledge but of my God. I did not know my way around the Prayer Book or the Bible, my prayers were very rudimentary and I had little insight into what was happening to me. Yet God called me in my foolishness. I cannot understand to this day how I was chosen from among the bright students and well-qualified men to go to Kelham College. God certainly was at work in a mysterious way.

Patrick was born somewhere near the west coast of the Roman Province of Britannia, most likely near one of the shortest sea crossings from Ireland. This would place his home anywhere from Wales up to the Antonine Wall. It has often been claimed that the Dumbarton area around the Clyde is a strong contender as his birthplace. It was the political capital of Strathclyde. A chieftain living on Dumbarton Rock, a twin peak of lava, was in an ideal position to defend the Clyde. When the Romans withdrew from Scotland in 410, Dumbarton Rock remained important, as it was named Dun Breatann, the fortress of the Britons. This was the name given to it by the Irish; the Britons had called it Alt Clut, the Rock of the Clyde. The biographer of St Patrick, Muirchu, says this fortress was the home of Coroticus, a British leader from whom Patrick demanded the release of Christian prisoners.

The only place name that St Patrick mentions is Bannavem Taburniae. There is no simple way of deciphering this name but it is now usually read as Banna Venta Berniae. This suggests a local market centre or a gateway near the fort of Banna in the hill country of Berniae or Bernicia. The Roman fort of Birdoswald on Hadrian's Wall was known as Banna and it is in the district of Bernicia. Birdoswald fits well as Banna, the gateway to the hill country. This area near Carlisle and Hadrian's Wall, where Ninian worked, is now thought to be the most likely birthplace of Patrick.

Patrick tells us his father was a Roman decurion, a local official, and that they kept a farm. He tells us that his family were Christians, in fact his father was a deacon in the Church and his grandfather was a priest. Once again we are hearing of early Christians of whom we hardly know anything. To learn that his grandfather was a priest tells again of Christian activity and no doubt a place of worship in the far reaches of the Empire. Tradition takes it even further back and it has been suggested that his great-grandfather was also a priest. At least we know that Patrick came from two generations of clergy.

When Patrick was almost 16, he was captured by a raiding party from Ireland and sold to the king in Armagh. In an instant, all the privileges of home, security of position and hopes for the future disappeared. It would seem he was a typical child of a priestly family. He had not taken much notice of his faith until there was a danger that it was to be taken from him. Somehow he met up with fellow Christians, most likely also captives from among the Britons, and from them not only did he gain new courage but his faith grew. The *Confession* begins:

> I, Patrick, a sinner, the rudest and least among all the faithful, and most contemptible to many, had for my father, Calpornius, a deacon, a son of Potitus a presbyter, who dwelt in the village of Bannavem Taburniae, for he had a small farm hard by the place where I was taken captive. I was then nearly sixteen years of age. I did not know the true God: and I was taken to Ireland in captivity with so many thousand men, in accordance with our deserts, and we kept not His precepts, and were not obedient to our priests, who admonished us for our salvation.
>
> (*Confession*, § 1)

We learn immediately that Patrick was not the only Christian captive and that he came from an area that had priests to look after the Christian communities. When Patrick says he 'did not know the true God', we have to understand it in the same way that he calls himself the least of all the faithful. Perhaps, like many a son or daughter of a clerical family, he sought not to follow too closely the way of his father and grandfather. There can be little doubt that the influence of his Christian home, once taken for granted, did bear a strong influence on his later life. Patrick saw not only himself as an apostate, but many of those who were taken prisoner with him. They were Christian slaves in a heathen land, though there were Christians among the people of Ireland. As Joseph, sold into slavery in Egypt brought benefit to that land and the land of his ancestors, so it is with St Patrick. Out of what seemed to be a great tragedy, God, through Patrick, brought goodness. Patrick looking back on this exclaims:

> I know this most certainly, that before I was humbled I was like a stone lying in deep mud; and He who is mighty came, and in his own mercy raised me, and lifted me up, and placed me on top of the wall. And hence I ought loudly to cry out to the Lord, to return also something to the Lord for all His so great benefits, here and in eternity, which benefits the minds of men cannot estimate.
>
> (*Confession*, § 12)

There is no doubt that the young Patrick was encouraged by the faithful in their captivity. Like many groups before them and after them, their faith gave them solidarity and a hope in their troubles. When all help around them seemed to have disappeared they had little option but to put their trust in the Lord. Sometimes life needs to be stripped bare before we realize where our help and our support really comes from: it takes some event to awaken us to the presence of our God. In our prosperous world we tend to put our trust in our own might and in our own planning. We believe that we are able to be self-sufficient and to not often need to have recourse to God. Yet one day, every one of us will discover that we have no power of ourselves to help ourselves, and we will need to put our trust in the love and in the power of God. No one can escape the final captivities of weakness and death, without help from the Almighty. Towards the end of the *Confession* Patrick writes:

> I may pour out my blood for His name's sake, even although I myself may even be deprived of burial, and my corpse torn limb from limb by dogs or wild beasts, or that the fowls of heaven should devour it. I believe most certainly that if this should happen to me, I shall have gained both soul and body. Because without any doubt we shall rise in that day in the brightness of the sun, that is in the glory of Jesus Christ our Redeemer, as sons of the living God, and joint heirs with Christ, and to be conformable to his image, for of Him, and in Him and through Him we shall reign.
>
> (*Confession*, § 59)

Patrick knew the dangers of the life he was leading from the moment he was taken away from home as a slave until he died, but through his captivity his faith was deepened and enriched. Patrick was weak but his God was mighty: the future was unknown but Patrick knew who went with him. Patrick time and again experienced,

> Peace, perfect peace, our future all unknown?
> Jesus we know and he is on the throne.
>
> (Harry Bickersteth, 1825–1906)

The same confidence in God is expressed in a modern prayer by Desmond Tutu:

Goodness is stronger than evil:
Love is stronger than hate;
Light is stronger than darkness;
Life is stronger than death;
Victory is ours through Him who loves us.

(Tutu, 1995, p. 80)

The Breastplate of St Patrick, though not likely written by him, does express his trust in the God who calls him:

Against the demon snares of sin,
The vice that gives temptation force,
The natural lusts that war within,
The hostile men that mar my course –
Or few or many, far or nigh,
In every place and in all hours,
Against their fierce hostility,
I bind to me these holy powers.

Against all Satan's spell and wiles,
Against false words of heresy,
Against the knowledge that defiles,
Against the heart's idolatry,
Against the wizard's evil craft,
Against the death-wound and the burning,
The choking wave, the poison'd shaft,
Protect me, Christ, till Thy returning.

(trans. Mrs Alexander)

Patrick alone on the hillsides of Ireland was given opportunity to be open to his God:

But after I had come to Ireland I used to daily feed cattle, and I prayed frequently during the day: the love of God and the fear of Him increased more and more, and faith became stronger, and the spirit was stirred; so that in one day I said about a hundred prayers, and in the night nearly the same; so that I used even to remain in the woods and in the mountain; before daylight I used to rise to prayer, through snow, through frost, through rain, and felt no harm; nor was there any slothfulness in me, as I now perceive, because the spirit was then fervent within me.

(*Confession*, § 16)

Patrick was building up his relationship with God by turning to him at least a hundred times each day, and the same at night. By being enforced to live on the hillsides Patrick was given the opportunity to converse with God and to become aware of the presence and power of God in his life. He discovered he was not alone and not forsaken, for God was ever there. The same God is with each of us; if we do not know his presence it is perhaps because we have not sought it out. Faith is not about what we believe, it is about our relationship with God. Our God seeks a personal relationship with each of us, and we cannot have that relationship if we do not spend time with him, talking to him and listening to him.

When I was 15 I left a grammar school and went to work down a coal-mine. I was soon on my own, tending a conveyor belt in the depths of the earth. There was much noise but there was also solitude and the lack of human voices. Here with fossilized creatures above me and coal all around me was a great emptiness. It was that lack of conversation, the removal of myself from the nearness of others, that increased my awareness of the mysteries that were about me, and the great mystery who is God. In the silence God was at last given the opportunity to approach me. I am sure

the same happened to the young Patrick as he tended
the sheep. This awareness would bring me out of the
darkness and set me on a course to train for ministry. I
would later love to recite Psalm 40 in a bright College
chapel and say, 'he brought me also out of the horrible
pit, out of the mire and clay: and set my feet upon the
rock, and ordered my goings' (Psalm 40.2, Book of
Common Prayer). Patrick the slave would become a
slave for Christ's sake, and I would return to a mining
area to begin my ministry. I actually worked underground one day a week as a chaplain for the National
Coal Board.

The mine taught me silence. When I went to
Kelham, I was plunged into silence every day from
9.30 p.m. until 9.30 a.m. and even then silence was
not relaxed fully until lunchtime. Often I heard these
words from the College Principles:

> The conversation of the brethren should help and cheer
> us, but God's voice speaks most often in silence.

> Keep some part of every day free from all noise and the
> voices of men, for human distraction and the craving for
> it hinder Divine Peace.

> He who cannot keep silence is not contented with God.

Martin sought to enter silence by being a hermit.
Ninian had his cave on the shore to retreat to. Patrick
virtually had silence forced upon him. Silence and
solitude reveal to us new depths within ourselves
and within the world. Withdrawal from people
actually helps us to appreciate them and to be more
attentive to them.

In our times silence is often banished, our senses are bombarded with noise, by visual and auditory stimuli. Many churches have become like the world and have no space for stillness: the Word of God cannot find room! We need to create times and places of stillness. Silence carves us out, as a bowl is carved out, that we may be able to have room for our God, that we may discover we dwell in him and he in us. Silence is part of any act of love or adoration, far richer than words and opens our heart to the other. Pilgrimage for the love of God begins when we are brave enough to enter into silence. Teresa of Avila said, 'Settle upon Him in solitude and you will come upon him in yourself.' One of the greatest treasures of learning that I ever received from Kelham was the gift of silence: in the silence we can enthuse in our God.

Patrick expresses his enthusiasm for God in the words, 'the spirit was then fervent within me'. In a few words we get a glimpse of the thrill and the joy of being a Christian and the power it brings to one's life. Patrick was becoming aware that he was in God. The Greek for this is *en Theou* and from it we get our word enthusiasm. Patrick later says, 'I saw him praying in me, and he was as it were within my body, and I heard him above me' (*Confession*, § 25). He then talks about how the Spirit of God works within each of us. Throughout his life, Patrick seeks to tell us how we dwell in God and God dwells in us. Much later when the daughters of the king of Connaught ask, 'Who is your God and where is He?' Patrick fervent in spirit replied:

Our God is the God of all, the God of Heaven
and earth, sea and river.
He has his dwelling in heaven and earth and sea
and all that are therein.
He inspires all things. He quickens all things.
He kindles the light of the sun and of the moon.
He has a Son co-eternal with Himself and like
unto Him.
And the Holy Spirit breathes in them.
Father Son and Holy Spirit, they are not divided.
I desire to unite you to the Son of the Heavenly,
For you are daughters of a king of earth.

Patrick's love for God is expressed in a trinitarian
formula, but in fact it is his experience of the Sacred
Three that makes him speak this way: it is the person
who lives the life that understands the theology of the
Trinity. Patrick was in no doubt that

The Father created us out of His love
and for His love.
The Son redeemed us by His love
and for His love.
The Spirit sustains us with his love
and for his love.
The Holy Three seek us in love
and for love.

Patrick says in the *Confession*:

In measure, therefore, of the faith of the Trinity it
behoves me to distinguish without shrinking from
danger, to make known the gift of God, and His everlasting consolation and without fear to spread faithfully
everywhere the name of God, in order that even after my

death I may leave it as a bequest to my brethren, and to my sons, whom I have baptised in the Lord – so many thousand men.

(Confession, § 14)

Patrick was baptizing in the Name of the Trinity and preaching in the Name of the Trinity. It is not surprising the 'Breastplate' attributed to him begins

> I bind unto myself today
> The Strong name of the Trinity,
> By invocation of the same,
> The Three in One, and one in Three.

Patrick and the Church in the Celtic lands saw that they were ever in the presence of the Sacred Three. On rising in the morning the people of the Hebrides would say:

> I am bending my knee
> In the eye of the Father who created me,
> In the eye of the Son who purchased me,
> In the eye of the Spirit who cleansed me,
> In friendship and affection.

(Carmichael, 1983, p. 3)

There were similar trinitarian prayers for work and journeying, for the home and for sleeping: the whole day was in the presence of the Trinity. God is ever with us.

There is no place where God is not to be found. If you banish God from your life or even a portion of it, you cease to deal with reality or with the true depths of the world and your own being. Any true perspective of the world needs to acknowledge mystery and awe. We may not want to put conventional names to our awareness, because such names have been greatly misused, but the reality is still there. To deny mystery and awe any entry into our lives is to impoverish ourselves, and the world around us. There is a great joy in being able to awaken to the presence. Life becomes so much richer if we discover that we dwell in God and he is in us. Patrick would have understood the words of Julian of Norwich that are so hard to understand by many today: 'You are more in heaven than on earth.' If this is not part of our experience, is it not because we have ceased to keep up a vital relationship with our creator, redeemer and sustainer? We have so many wonderful things we can do in this world we are always tempted to forget that our God seeks a relationship with us. God is not a Sunday exercise, nor a recreational option, God is life and health: God is not for debate or analysis, or to be proved; God is to be encountered and to be known. When we come out of our safety and walk the edges of our experience we open our lives to the living God. Here are some words of William Temple I heard at a diocesan conference. I hope they challenge you as much as they do me:

> Throw off what hampers your service, even though it be venerable with the history of ages, or consecrated by dear familiarity. Use these things as aids to service if you can, but if they are only clogs cut them off and cast them from you. The day is come that burns like fire, for Christ has cast his fire on earth. Come out from your safety and comfort, come out from your habits and conventions, listen for the voice of the wind as it sweeps over the world and stand where you may be caught in its onward rush.

The wilderness experience of Patrick made him give attention to God and to rejoice in his presence. His use of many prayers a day suggests a similar use of prayer to that of Cassian, who died about the year that Patrick was taken into captivity. Cassian gives this advice for continuous prayer:

> To preserve a continual recollection of God, keep these holy words always before you: 'O God, make speed to save me: O Lord make haste to help me' (Psalm 70.1).
>
> I am attacked by the passion of gluttony: I must say at once, 'O God, make speed to save me: O Lord make haste to help me'. I try to read but am overcome with a headache: I must call out, 'O God, make speed to save me: O Lord make haste to help me.' I am afflicted by insomnia: as I sigh and groan, I must pray, 'O God, make speed to save me: O Lord make haste to help me.' I have gained the grace of humility and simplicity: to keep myself from growing conceited, I must cry with all my strength, 'O God, make speed to save me: O Lord make haste to help me.'
>
> This verse should be our constant prayer: in adversity that we may be delivered, in prosperity that we may be kept safe and not fall a victim to pride. Let this verse be the unremitting occupation of your heart. At work in every task, on a journey, do not cease to repeat it. Meditate on these words as you drop off into slumber: through incessant use, grow accustomed to repeat them even when you sleep; and let them be the first words when you awake; let them accompany you all the day long.
>
> (Every *et al.*, 1984, p. 6)

It is good to note that this form of prayer is to be an 'occupation of the heart': it is not just repeating things and hoping to believe them, it is not 'positive thinking': so often positive thinking can be positively stupid. This way of praying is putting us in touch with the reality that is, the reality of the presence and power of God: that God is with us and cares for us. If we neglect this worship of the heart, all of our prayer life becomes a struggle. It is the heart that gives life to our prayers, when that heart is full of God and his love. Archbishop Anthony Bloom writes: 'One of the reasons why communal worship or private prayer seem to be so dead or so conventional is that the act of worship, which takes place in the heart communing with God, is too often missing' (Bloom, 1966, p. vii).

Whilst at College I learnt the great richness in having only a few words in prayer. God knows our every need and he does not require us to inform him of what is going on in the world or in our lives. He is already open to us and our prayers; what God requires is that we open ourselves to him and let him have a living relationship with us. The mind will not remain empty but will wander all over the place, so it is good to have a few words that will keep it in check and quiet before the presence. I started with the sentence, 'Lord, Jesus Christ, Son of God have mercy upon me a sinner.' As my prayer time developed the sentence got shorter and I was happy to be there in the presence of our God. Sometimes the sentence took an hour to pray. Sometimes I only used the word 'Lord' as I enthused in the presence. At times when it was hard to pray, I repeated the sentence quietly and let each word vibrate with its own reality. At all times this was a love relationship with my God, so in many ways the words did not matter, it was my attitude and approach in love that was important.

Though prayer and the awareness of God kept Patrick full of hope, it did not prevent him from having the desire to escape his captors. Patrick, a free-born Roman citizen, could not have been content to accept slavery. It is important to realize that Patrick was taken away from a civilized country to a country that was just emerging from the Iron Age. As Patrick knew the comforts of Roman Britain, where there were roads between cities, where houses often had paved floors, plumbing and baths, the captivity by a tribal chief with a primitive lifestyle must have been difficult to bear.

Escape would incur risk and danger, if not death, but if the opportunity arose Patrick would need to grasp it. Yet it was in the years he was captive that Patrick found a greater freedom, for his spirit was set free to worship in ways he had not experienced before. He was beginning to be a slave to him whose service is perfect freedom. Patrick would well understand the words of the hymn writer George Matheson:

> Make me a captive, Lord
> And then I shall be free.

Like many another, Patrick sought ways of escape from his captivity in Ireland, and waited until the opportunity came. Patrick remained a slave for six years before he dreamed of a way to escape. His escape route would take him 200 miles across country and to a ship that took him to strange lands. After many adventures, including near starvation, Patrick returned to his family. There must have been great rejoicing in his home on his return, and to discover he was such a dedicated Christian. Perhaps it was his own clerical family that persuaded him to be prepared for ordination. The man taken as a slave to Ireland gained his freedom to become a voluntary slave of Christ and later he would return to that land to serve his new Master.

There was some time spent in Gaul at this stage in Patrick's life and perhaps even at Rome, but all is very vague and we cannot be certain where he went or where he was trained. His training for the priesthood certainly included learning the Bible, for he knew much of it by heart. Again the emphasis is by heart: the Scriptures would be learnt in worship as much as in study, and they would be learnt in the several daily services of each day.

When I was training for the ministry, I attended five services in the chapel every day, and at all of these services we said Psalms. The whole of the Psalter was said through every month and some Psalms were said every day, including Psalm 119! The Psalms were said slowly and rhythmically so that we could meditate upon them. By the time I left college I knew all the Psalms by heart, and also the Collects, Epistles and Gospels for every Sunday of the year. This was a great resource that I could call on at any time, especially in times of need or spiritual dryness. I could recite the Psalms when travelling without the need of a book, though sometimes not without a little prompting. This is a great way of learning, for it is a learning by heart that influences the way you communicate what you have learnt.

Patrick's education was quite rudimentary. More than once he regrets the lack of a 'higher education':

his own writings are really quite rough and rustic in nature, but we must remember it was in an age when hardly anyone could read or write. By necessity Patrick had to learn by heart what he wanted to tell to other people. These saints were not people of the Book so much as people of the presence, they spoke of God whom they loved and served.

After his captivity it is natural that his parents did not want him to leave them again. Patrick, however, was sure of a calling. His captivity in Ireland had been for a purpose. He heard in a dream the voice of those in Ireland who were near the wood of Foclut, which is close by the Western Sea, crying out, 'We entreat you holy youth, that you come and walk among us.' Patrick, knowing this would entail many dangers, made his way to Ireland and to begin his battle to win a nation for Christ.

The story of his encounter with the high king at Tara may not be so much a factual story as a tale to tell of Patrick's battle to bring the light of Christ to a people that walked in darkness. Some scholars think the whole story of the Tara encounter was written to be told at the Easter Ceremonies, a time when we pray 'May the Christ risen in glory scatter the darkness from our hearts and our minds.' Even in the twenty-first century, after sitting in the dark and longing for the dawn, there is something powerful about the Easter Fire. On Lindisfarne on Holy Saturday we meet in church in the dark; we stay there and listen to promises for about an hour. Then we go out of church down a rocky road: life is often like a downhill rocky road! As we arrive at the beach near the church there is a great fire waiting for us. We do not light the fire, it is as ever waiting for us to come to it. From this fire, nearly getting scorched, I light the large Easter candle saying, 'Alleluia, Christ is risen' and all reply 'He is risen indeed, Alleluia.' We came down in silence to this fire, we will return to church singing. From the Easter candle every person will receive a light, until the darkness is dispersed and the church filled with the glow from each individual.

Tara was said to be the 'centre of witchcraft and idolatry in Ireland'. Here was where the Christian faith would confront the old ways, and in the person of Patrick seek to triumph over darkness. There was also a deep understanding that if the leaders of the people were not persuaded to accept the faith it would be hard to keep their subjects faithful. The story is made to fit Easter and the Easter Fire. When Easter approached, Patrick was determined to keep the festival at Tara: the great festival of the Risen Lord was a time to rise over the heathen. The time when the heathen were being plunged into darkness was the time to bring them into the Light of Christ. In a similar vein we today proclaim, 'May the Christ risen in glory scatter the darkness from our hearts and our minds.' It was the same Light of Christ that Patrick brought to Ireland to bring them out of their darkness to his glorious light.

The time chosen by Patrick was also the time of the great pagan festival at Tara: all lights were to be extinguished, all fires were to be put out. The king would provide fire for his people and bring them light, they were to be dependent on him for warmth and light. The extinguishing of all fires showed their allegiance and dependency as well as the king's power;

to disobey meant death because of their rebellion. Patrick understood all this, yet he and his companions collected firewood and built a great bonfire. They lit the Easter Fire, which lit up the whole of the area of Mag Breg. The king enquired who dared to disobey him and to light a fire. The king's wise men knew who it was and warned him that if this fire was not put out immediately it would flood Ireland with its light and burn until Doomsday. They said of Patrick: 'He goes around the Munster men and preaches to them and baptizes them and leaves them clerics and churches.' The old religion was under threat and they said, 'This is the shaven head and the falsifier who is deceiving everyone. Let us go and attack him and see if his God will help him.'

The king was sure that Patrick had to be stopped, so he said, 'We will go and slay the man who has kindled this fire.' In the eyes of Patrick, the powers of darkness were now set against the children of light. Soldiers were sent to capture Patrick and to prevent him from freely approaching Tara: they were said to have surrounded Patrick and his men. Patrick and his companions somehow escaped their attackers; they came to no harm and they entered Tara. Patrick said, 'Some boast of chariots, and some of horses: but we boast of the name of the LORD our God.' This quotation from Psalm 20.7 is alluding to the Exodus and the children of Israel escaping slavery to enter the Promised Land.

Whatever the approach, the Christian faith was being accepted without great opposition in Ireland; it appears the people were ready for a new and vital faith. The people were being convinced that this new faith was more powerful than their old religion. Tradition says that it was at this time that Patrick composed the hymn known as the 'Deer's Cry' or 'St Patrick's Breastplate'. Though the prayer may have been written well after Patrick's death, it expresses well much of the early Celtic Christian faith. It is full of a God who surrounds us, a Christ who is about us, and the Spirit that is within us: it affirms the glory of God woven into all of creation like a fine thread, a presence and a power that pervades all things. Today the same presence, the same light of God, is to be found by all who will open their eyes, their ears, their minds and their hearts. This presence is not something we create but is there waiting to be revealed: it is God's gift of himself to us. Let us enjoy our God, his presence and his power, through the words attributed to Patrick:

> I arise today
> Through a mighty strength, the invocation of the
>   Trinity,
> Through belief in the threeness,
> Through confession of the oneness
> Of the Creator of Creation.
>
> I arise today
> Through the strength of Christ's birth with his
>   baptism,
> Through the strength of his crucifixion with his
>   burial,
> Through the strength of his resurrection with his
>   ascension,
> Through the strength of his descent for the
>   judgement of Doom.

I arise today
Through the strength of the love of the Cherubim,
In the obedience of angels,
In the service of archangels,
In the hope of resurrection to meet with reward,
In the prayers of the patriarchs,
In prediction of the prophets,
In preaching of apostles,
In faith of confessors,
In innocence of holy virgins,
In deeds of righteous men.

I arise today
Through the strength of heaven;
Light of sun,
Radiance of moon,
Splendour of fire,
Speed of lightning,
Swiftness of wind,
Depth of sea,
Stability of earth,
Firmness of rock.

I arise today
Through God's strength to pilot me:
God's might to uphold me,
God's wisdom to guide me,
God's eye to look before me,
God's ear to hear me,
God's word to speak to me,
God's hand to guard me,
God's way to lie before me,
God's shield to protect me,
God's host to save me,
From snares of devils,
From temptations of vices

From every one who shall wish me ill,
Afar and anear,
Alone and in a multitude.

I summon today all these powers between me and
    those evils,
Against every cruel merciless power that may oppose
    my body and soul,
Against incantations of false prophets,
Against black laws of pagandom,
Against false laws of heretics,
Against craft of idolatry,
Against spells of women and smiths and wizards,
Against every knowledge that corrupts man's
    body and souls.

Christ to shield me today
Against poisoning, against burning,
Against drowning, against wounding,
So there may come to me abundance of reward.
Christ with me, Christ before me, Christ behind me,
Christ in me, Christ beneath me, Christ above me,
Christ on my right, Christ on my left,
Christ when I lie down, Christ when I sit down,
Christ when I arise,
Christ in the heart of every man who thinks of me,
Christ in the mouth of every one who speaks of me,
Christ in every eye that sees me,
Christ in every ear that hears me.

I arise today
Through a mighty strength,
The invocation of the Trinity,
Through belief in the threeness,
Through confession of the oneness
Of the Creator of Creation.

(Meyer, 1928)

In the Irish preface to this hymn found in the *Liber Hymnorum*, Trinity College Dublin, comes the following promise:

> Patrick made this hymn. In the time of Loegaire, son of Niall, it was made. Now the cause of making it was to protect himself with his monks, against the deadly enemies who were in ambush against the clerics. And this is a corslet of faith for the protection of body and souls against devils and human beings and vices. Whosoever will sing it every day, with pious meditation on God, devils will not stay before him. It will be a safeguard to him against all poison and envy. It will be a defence to him against sudden death.
>
> (Wright, 1889, p. 120)

This was not a belief in magic but an assertion that nothing will separate us from the love of God in Christ Jesus. Not a protection from these things happening but a protection from them destroying us forever; declaring that in God we are more than conquerors. I prayed this prayer every day for over a year to affirm the presence and the power of God and that God works through his creation.

After the Tara episode, Patrick worked mainly in the North of Ireland, and encouraged many of the converts to become monks and nuns. As he set out on this venture he is reported to have said: 'I will go that I may show my readiness before the men of Ireland. It is not a candle under a vat that I will make myself.' He wandered all over, preaching, baptizing and building churches. However, all was not plain sailing for this early church. In his other writing 'The Letter to Coroticus' he admonishes a Christian whom he describes as an 'apostate Pict'. Coroticus and his soldiers had captured slaves from Ireland who had been recently converted to Christianity and they had taken them back across the Irish Sea to sell or to hold for ransom. Patrick, anxious for these young men and women, asks the Christian Coroticus to set them free, and when he does not Patrick prayed that the chief should be 'banished from this world and the next'. Obviously not all converts remained loyal to their leaders.

Whatever their hardships, these leaders believed they were not left on their own: they would have often recited the words of the Psalmist:

> If it had not been the LORD who was on our side, let
> Israel now say –
> if it had not been the LORD who was on our side,
> when men rose up against us,
> then they would have swallowed us up alive,
> when their anger was kindled against us;
> then the flood would have swept us away,
> the torrent would have gone over us,
> then over us would have gone raging waters.
> Blessed be the LORD, who has not given us as prey to
> their teeth!
> We have escaped as a bird from the snare of the
> fowlers;
> the snare is broken, and we have escaped!
> Our help is in the name of the LORD, who made
> heaven and earth.

> (Psalm 124)

If we do not know the reality of these words, it could be that we have never pondered them in our heart.

Patrick had been called to serve on what was thought to be the very edge of the world and among barbarians. His life was often at risk from enemies and from a new captivity and slavery. As an old man, Patrick, near the end of the *Confession*, writes

> I daily expect either murder, or to be circumvented, or to be reduced to slavery, or mishap of some kind ... I fear none of these things on account of the promises of heaven; for I have cast myself into the hands of the Omnipotent God, who rules everywhere, as saith the prophet, 'Cast thy thought on the Lord, and He will sustain thee.' Behold now, I commend my soul to my most faithful God.

> (*Confession*, §§ 55–6)

The slave of Christ trusts fully in the God who commands him and gives his life purpose and meaning. Patrick was not afraid to walk the edge of the world, for in so doing he was sure he would be enabled to step into the greater presence and peace of his God.

Exercises

1 'If you want (prayer) to be pure, right and enjoyable, you must choose some sort of prayer consisting of few but forcible words and repeat it frequently for a long while. Then you will find delight in prayer' (*The Way of a Pilgrim*).

   Select a short sentence and learn to pray with the lips, with the mind, with the heart.

2 Pray slowly, seeking to spend much time on each line:

I bind unto myself today
The strong name of the Trinity,
By invocation of the same,
The Three in One and One in Three.

Christ be with me
Christ be before me
Christ be behind me
Christ be above me
Christ be beneath me
Christ at my right hand
Christ at my left hand
Christ this day within
Christ and about me.

3 Read Psalm 91 each day for a week and make its affirmations your own. Or take these words to heart on alternate days to the Psalm:

Christ as a light
Illumine and guide me!
Christ as a shield overshadow and cover me!
Christ be under me! Christ be over me!
Christ be beside me,
On left hand and right!
Christ be before me, behind me, about me!
Christ this day, be within and without me!
Christ the lowly and meek,
Christ the all-powerful, be
In the heart of each to whom I speak,
In the mouth of each who speaks to me,
In all who draw near me,
Or see me, or hear me!

Oswald the Open Handed

Above the town of Hexham on Hadrian's Wall is the small village with the name of Wall. It is in an area that was once called Heavenfield and not far from the site of a decisive battle in the seventh century. Today at Wall, standing in a field and approached by a line of sycamore trees, is the little church of St Oswald-in-Lee. From this elevated place you can look out over a wide expanse of Northumberland; there is more than the eye can take in at one time. Cheviot itself is in the distance, speaking of another border. By the roadside before you enter the field with the church is a stone cross – pity it is not a wooden one – commemorating a great battle for a kingdom. It was more than an earthly battle, for it was a battle for the hearts and minds of the people. A battle fought by the exiled Oswald in 643, for the kingdom of his father and to win it for his Father in heaven.

Oswald was said to have descended from the pagan god Woden, or Odin. His name means 'Divine Ruler' but the god it was related to was Woden.

Oswald was supposed to have been the twelfth generation descended from this pagan god that gives his
name to Wednesday. Oswald, though born a pagan,
was to become a Christian ruler. His life has all
the romance of folk legend, such as the tale of the
fictitious Beowulf. Oswald would seek to conquer
the powers of darkness in the land and to bring a new
freedom to the people. For a brief eight years Oswald
was the leader of his people, and though he would
be cut down in battle his achievements were such
that he is remembered when other warrior kings are
forgotten. Whereas most saints are churchmen and
women, professional religious, monks, nuns, bishops
and hermits, Oswald belongs to a select band of royal
saints and is the first Anglo-Saxon saint to have
widespread recognition beyond his own country.
Bede gives Oswald the title of 'Most holy and most
victorious, king of Northumbria'.

As a child I used to visit Bamburgh and look upon
the castle in wonder. I knew from my father that
Oswald had a fortress where the present castle stands.
As I walked the splendid beach below the castle, I
would imagine setting out in battle along the sands: it
would have been good to be able to join such a mighty
king. Only later in life did I realize how awful it
could have been! From the sands we would go into
Bamburgh church: here in the church of St Peter the
incorrupt arm of Oswald used to be enshrined. My
father told me Oswald's head was in the same coffin as
Cuthbert's body in Durham Cathedral. As a child this
spreading of the saint's body as relics was quite a fascination. My father described Oswald as 'a good and
generous king and the man who brought Aidan from

Iona'. For a youngster this is the stuff real stories are made of, and it fired my imagination.

As the son of a king, Oswald grew up in the palace with his brothers Eanfrith and Oswy and his sister Ebba. The kingdoms were small and relatively new, having little stability. Oswald's father, Aethelfrith, had taken over the kingdom to the south, Deira, and united it with his own Bernicia, and so laid the foundation of Northumbria. During this time many of the indigenous Britons had been forced off their land, made captives or killed. Aethelfrith managed to transform what had been a small war party into the mightiest military power in Northern Britain: it was ruled by might and very dependent on the sword. Bede writes concerning Aethelfrith (also known as Ethelfrid):

> During this period Ethelfrid, a very powerful and ambitious king, ruled the kingdom of Northumbria. He ravaged the Britons more cruelly than all other English leaders, so that he might well be compared to Saul the King of Israel, except that he was ignorant of true religion. He overran a greater area than any other kings or chiefs, exterminating or enslaving the inhabitants, extorting tribute, and annexing their lands for the English.
>
> (Bede, *History*, Book 1, ch. 34,
> Sherley-Price, 1955, p. 92)

Obviously at this stage what was going on is what we now politely call 'ethnic cleansing'. At least one if not two of Aethelfrith's ancestors was called 'The Flame Bearer', not because they brought light, but because they destroyed villages and their communities by fire. The local Britons were often forced to hide in the hill country away from the occupied coastlands. Amongst the persecuted were Christians who lived in the area before Aidan arrived, and like many persecuted peoples throughout the ages they fled to the remoter hill country to escape being killed. A Christian king, Urien ap Rheged, was killed at Lindisfarne trying to drive out the pagan ancestors of Oswald.

Aethelfrith was defeated and killed by Raedwald, perhaps by the very sword that is in the Sutton Hoo collection in the new centre at Sutton Hoo. In 616 Edwin took over the kingdom of Northumbria, and all Aethelfrith's children went into exile for their safety; they all went to the north. The oldest of these children, Eanfrith, married a Pictish princess and his son Tallorcan became the king of the Picts. It appears that Oswald, Oswy and their sister Ebba went to the west coast of Scotland to what was the Irish Celtic kingdom of Dalriada, in what is now Argyll. At this time Oswald, who was 12 years old, along with his brother and sister, was given a Christian education. It is thought that the boys spent at least some time with the monks on the island of Iona. Ebba was more likely to be educated on the nearby 'Island of Women', Eilean non Ban.

As Oswald grew, it was essential that he learnt the art of warfare, so that when the time was right he could claim back the kingdom of his father. Oswald probably spent a good deal of time at the stronghold of Dunadd, being trained in weaponry and warfare. The exile was to be quite a long one, for it was 17 years before Oswald got the opportunity to return to Northumbria. Edwin was killed at the battle of Hatfield Chase by the alliance of Penda of Mercia and

Cadwallon of Gwynedd in the year 632. Eanfrith came southwards to claim his heritage with 12 thanes and a British–Celtic war-band, hoping to make a new alliance with the Christian British leader Cadwallon. Though Eanfrith came to seek peace, Cadwallon was not willing to deal with the children of Aethelfrith, whom he saw as a twister and a cheat, a killer of the indigenous peoples. Eanfrith and his men were put to the sword. Hopes for an easy return to Northumbria were shattered.

When news reached Oswald of his brother's death, he prepared an army to come and march against Penda and Cadwallon: this army was much smaller than the opposition as many of the fighting men had already been killed along with Eanfrith. Any chance of Oswald being victorious was slender; common sense would have told him to stay in the north until he could muster a greater army.

The battle was to take place near the land called Heavenfield at a place called the Deniseburn. At Heavenfield, Oswald and his army set up camp and waited; they needed to restore their energies after their march south. It was in December, and the cold night air with its clear sky was testing enough for both sides. In the forest below and towards the river Tyne there were wild beasts; the enemy would come from this direction unless Oswald marched to meet them. The mist rose in the valley, and the troops tried to sleep. As Oswald slept, he had a vision of St Columba of Iona coming to him and speaking with him. It may have been that Oswald had brought a relic of Columba with him. Columba told Oswald that he and the smaller army would be victorious. Columba then reminded him of God speaking to Joshua at the river Jordan and just before entering the Promised Land: 'Be strong and of good courage. Behold I shall be with you. Be determined and confident for you will be the leader of these people as they occupy this land.' Then the saint added, 'March out this following night from your camp to battle, for on this occasion the Lord has granted to me that your foes will be put to flight.' As the armies did not usually fight at night it was perhaps the early dawn attack that would give Oswald the advantage. Oswald knew the odds were against him and if he won it was due to the strength that God gave. This event is interesting in the way it tells us of the reverence Oswald had for the founder of Iona and also for his own knowledge of the Scriptures. Obviously, Oswald had received a proper Christian education. At the same time the details make us aware that Oswald planned his campaign and used a surprise attack to gain advantage.

There is an affirmation attributed to Columba which would well suit Oswald on this occasion:

> Alone with none but Thee, my God,
> I journey on my way;
> What need I fear when Thou art near,
> O King of night and day?
> More safe I am within Thy hand
> Than if a host did round me stand.
>
> My destined time is fixed by Thee,
> and death doth know his hour.
> Did warriors strong around me throng,
> they could not stay his power;
> no walls of stone can man defend
> when Thou Thy messenger dost send.

My life I yield to Thy decree,
and bow to Thy control
in peaceful calm, for from Thine arm
no power can wrest my soul.
Could earthly omen e'er appal
a man that heeds the heavenly call!

The child of God can fear no ill,
His chosen dread no foe;
we leave our fate with Thee and wait
Thy bidding when we go.
'Tis not from chance our comfort springs,
Thou art our trust, O King of kings.

(Whiteside, 1997, pp. 52–3)

Columba is said to have won a great battle in Ireland and there is no doubt stories of his life inspired this future king.

Whilst at Iona, Oswald will have also heard of the vision of the young Emperor Constantine and the promise the Emperor had of being able to conquer. As Constantine was preparing for battle he had a dream, or a vision, in which God sent him a miraculous sign. It was in the afternoon and the sun was sinking towards the horizon, when Constantine saw in the sky above the sun, a cross with this inscription attached: TOUTW NIKA (In this sign conquer). It was told him that the sign he saw was the Chi-Rho, the first two letters in Greek of the word 'Christ'. Constantine ordered that a jewelled replica of this sign was made for him, and that the sign should be placed on all the standards of the legions. In this sign Constantine's army moved forward to victory and he became one of the great leaders of Rome and a benefactor of the Church.

Oswald decided that before the battle, a cross should be raised and that his army should pray before it, praying that in this sign they might conquer the enemy. Two young trees were cut down and made into a rough cross; a hole was dug to stand it in. Oswald, full of his vision, seized the cross and held it with both hands in the hole until soil was piled around it so it stood upright. Oswald said, 'Let us all kneel before the Almighty, the everliving and true God, to defend us in his mercy from the proud enemy. He knows that the war we are engaged in is a just war and is for the deliverance of our people.' After this they quietly advanced on the enemy. Taken unawares, many of their foes scarcely had time to take up their swords, others fled in panic. The opposition was defeated and Cadwallon was slain. This battle ensured the country for the 'English'; the future of the Britons lay in being absorbed into the now settled invaders.

Oswald, no doubt, had promised that, if he survived and they were victorious, his kingdom would become Christian, in the same style as Constantine. This was a wise move, for it would please the indigenous Britons who had been oppressed for so long and many of whom were Christian. It would bring a unity to a divided nation and help to heal the wounds of the past. By now there was inter-marrying between the nations, so it was about time a new peace came to the kingdom. To help to bring this peace Oswald sent to Iona and the Celtic monks for help. To show how involved he was, when Aidan and his monks came to preach to the Northumbrians, Oswald gave them a place for their monastery and resources for building. More than this he gave himself, for in the early days, when Aidan needed an interpreter to speak to Oswald's people, the King himself took this role. This act must have helped the Christian greatly, for if the King was the interpreter, who could refuse to accept what was offered!

When it came to praying, the King himself set a good example to his people. Aidan's mission would not have had much success without the help of the King and his witness to the faith. At prayer it was noticed that Oswald sat with open hands palms upwards on his knees. It was said that Oswald often remained in prayer from the early hours of the service of Lauds until the dawn came. Bede tells us that on his death there was a proverb concerning Oswald which said, 'His life closed in prayer': for when he saw the enemy forces surrounding him and knew his end was near, he prayed for the souls of his soldiers as he fell saying, 'God have mercy on their souls.' The Anglo-Saxon kings were expected to be generous with their companions but tight-fisted with others. Oswald showed an open hand of welcome and generosity to many.

I cannot help but feel sorrow for those who are always tight-fisted: they are often punchy people. If you are tight-fisted, not only can you not give out, you cannot receive. I have illustrated this by asking people to clench their hands tight and then pick up the heap of coins I put before them. To be uptight is a form of stress. I offer you something to help you to relax:

Squeeze your fists tight closed until you can feel your fingers digging into your hands. Now curl your toes downwards until it hurts, screw up your face with eyes tight shut (not a pretty sight!). Let yourself relax, unclench your fists, uncurl your toes and bring a smile to your face. Already you have learnt one of the great secrets of life: you can make yourself more relaxed if you so choose. Make sure the rest of you follows suit, and check that you are relaxed in body, mind and spirit. Give yourself a rest.

Sit in a comfortable position. Gently close your hands, palms facing downwards. Now open your hands and let go of your troubles, fears, anxieties: drop them into the presence and the love of God. Let each go and do not pick them up again. If there is something troubling you give it to God; cast all your cares upon him for he cares for you. Say quietly:

> Calm me, O Lord, as you stilled the storm.
> Still me, O Lord, and keep me from harm.
> Let all the troubles within me cease.
> Enfold me, Lord, in your peace.

Or say:

> Bringing all my burdens, sorrow sin and care,
> At Thy feet I lay them and I leave them there.

After sitting in the stillness, turn the palms of your hands upwards and place them open on your knees. You are now open to receive. God is there and with you; accept his love, his joy, his peace. More than this, accept God himself into your life. Be open to the presence that is always there, that never leaves you.

As you are open to receive, now give to others. Share the peace, the love, the joy that God gives to you. Be relaxed in the presence of others and gently give them your time and attention. Know that you have moved from the uptight and tight-fisted to the open handed and the generous: give as God has given to you.

Oswald's open-handed actions showed in his generosity towards not only Aidan and the monks but also the poor. One Easter, Aidan had come to Bamburgh to dine with the King. The food was special as the Lenten fast was just over. A silver dish of rich food was set before them. Aidan was about to ask God's blessing upon the meal, when a nervous looking servant appeared in the doorway. He told the king that outside there was a great gathering of poor people. The winter had been hard and the people were starving. Their meagre resources had not seen them through to the growing season. Oswald stood up and pointing to the silver dish heavy laden with food demanded that it be taken out to the poor. 'Take this out and give them something to eat, and make sure that everyone gets something.' For a moment he paused as if in deep thought and then continued, 'And give them the silver dish the food is on: see that it is divided among them so that they all have something for another day.' The servant was amazed. He bowed to the king and then removed the great dish and its contents with the help of two other servants and began to distribute food and silver to the poor. Some believe that from this occasion began the giving of the Maundy Money by the sovereign. Aidan was deeply moved by this act of great generosity, and taking hold of the King's right hand exclaimed, 'May this hand never perish.' Bede tells that when Oswald's hand and arm were severed from his body after the battle, they were preserved and remained uncorrupted in the church of St Peter at Bamburgh.

Before what was to be his last battle, Oswald spent much time in prayer at Bamburgh. Once again, Penda was threatening the southern borders of Northumbria. Earthly kingdoms rise and fall, are so fragile and ever under threat. Oswald understood that his was a temporal kingdom and looked to his God and the kingdom that lasts forever. He also knew that his expedition to the south of Northumbria and beyond would be a dangerous one.

At first Oswald was successful and managed to drive Penda into Wales. However, such a force approaching the Welsh borders made the Welsh fear for their own safety and they joined forces with Penda. Oswald was almost caught off guard; he ought to have retreated but it was not in his nature to retreat. Oswald had lived a heroic life and if necessary he would die heroically. The enemy had called him 'Bright Blade', and he could not tarnish such a reputation by fleeing.

The ensuing battle was violent, as most battles are, and many good men died. The battle was going against the Northumbrians and Oswald's death was approaching. One by one the men of Oswald's army were slaughtered, until there was only a small band left protecting their king. This little group of valiant warriors made a human shield around their ruler, but were soon falling to sword and axe. Oswald knew the end was near and was ready to go over the edge of this world and walk with his Maker. Above the clamour of the sword and shield, Oswald raised his voice to pray for his men. His last words were, 'God have mercy on their souls.' At the age of 38 he was suddenly sent to his Maker and his heavenly home. It is said 'His life closed in prayer.'

Oswald's deeds became looked upon as the ideal for a Christian king. For a while it looked as if he might have become the patron saint of England, and an example for the new kingdoms of Europe, but with the coming of Cuthbert, Oswald ceased to be the most popular saint of the land.

Exercises

1 Oswald is remembered for his generosity, the giving not only of things but of himself. The hand of Oswald was not a clenched fist but an open hand, and for many he sought to change hostility into hospitality. How open handed are you? Are your actions and the actions of your life ones of welcome? Check out your acts of generosity and hospitality, and see where you can improve your open-handedness. Here are some words of Martin Luther that are worth thinking upon: 'If our goods are not available to the community they are stolen goods.' Practise the relaxing of your hands and the palms open exercise in this chapter.

2 Rejoice in the power, the protection and presence of God, using the words of Psalm 121:

> I lift up my eyes to the hills.
> From whence does my help come?
> My help comes from the LORD,
>   who made heaven and earth.
> He will not let your foot to be moved,
>   he who keeps you will not slumber.
> Behold, he who keeps Israel
>   will neither slumber nor sleep.
> The LORD is your keeper;

the LORD is your shade on your right hand.
The sun shall not smite you by day,
   nor the moon by night.
The LORD will keep you from all evil;
   he will keep your life.
The LORD will keep your going out and your
   coming in
   from this time forth and for evermore.

3 Affirm as a reality the words attributed to St Columba:

Alone with none but Thee, my God,
I journey on my way:
What need I fear if Thou art near,
O king of night and day?
More safe I am within Thy hand,
Than if a host did round me stand.

4 I would not like to think that Oswald was naïve enough to think 'God is on our side, so we cannot lose.' I would like to think it is an awareness like the words of Julian of Norwich:

He did not say, 'You shall not be tempest-tossed,
you shall not be work-weary,
you shall not be discomforted.'
But he said, 'You shall not be overcome.'
           (Julian of Norwich, 1980, p. 39)

A victory may be denied us, but the final outcome is assured: in him 'we are more than conquerors' (Romans 8.37). Take time to think this over.

Cuthbert and Seeing Beyond

In what is probably the oldest epic folk-tale from Ireland, *The Tain*, we get this wonderful encounter:

> 'What is your name?' Medb said to the girl.
> 'I am Fedelm, and I am a woman poet from
> Connacht.'
> 'Where have you come from?' Medb said.
> 'From learning verse and vision in Alba',
> the girl said.
> 'Have you the *imbas forasnai*, the Light of
> Foresight?' Medb said.
> 'Yes I have', the girl said.
> 'Then look for me and see what will become
> of my army.'
> So the girl looked.
>
> (Kinsella, 1970, pp. 60–1)

From early times there was the understanding that poetry was seeing the world in a different way, poetry was about vision and vision could be taught. If we do not see deeply and clearly it is because we have allowed our sight to become dimmed; we have closed our eyes to the wonders that are always about us. If we do not see how things are linked together in this world, it is because we have become insensitive to what is the reality of our situation. Our eyes are often dimmed because we have limited our vision to what we are willing to accept. Poetry is often used to link underlying relationships in a way that helps us to become aware of them. Words fail us when we are dealing with the deep mysteries of life, poetry attempts to bring us to an awareness of new depths and mysteries and help us see beyond where we think we are. Too often we are looking for God when he is with us. God is not absent, it is only our vision that is dim.

Many of the saints seem to have the ability to see beyond what is obvious and into a deeper and stranger world than most of us ever perceive. Cuthbert had this ability to see beyond from the time he was a child. There was an occasion when Cuthbert was suffering from a severe swelling of the knee and the sinews of his leg were contracting. His leg was extremely painful and he had to be carried outside because he was unable to walk. Cuthbert had been propped up against a wall in the sunshine. Looking into the distance Cuthbert saw shimmering light in the summer heat; there was a brightness approaching him. Soon the brightness took a more solid shape and Cuthbert saw a man on horseback. The man was dressed in white and looked extremely bright in the sunlight. He greeted Cuthbert with a blessing, 'God's peace and wholeness be upon you.' Cuthbert, unable to rise, felt ill at ease. 'Forgive me noble sir. If I was not lame on account of my sins I would arise and wait upon so noble a guest.' At these words the man descended from his horse and gave attention to Cuthbert's knee. He gave Cuthbert these instructions: 'Cook a pan of wheat flour in milk, until the wheat becomes a soft paste. Then put the paste on your knee whilst it is still hot.' The man mounted his horse and rode away. Cuthbert watched as the summer shimmering light and the man became one and at last the man disappeared in the hazy distance. Cuthbert wondered if it was a dream. By the time his friends came for him he was certain he had seen an angel on horseback. It was said of Cuthbert that in his times of need, he was never denied the help of angels.

In later life, when Cuthbert was the guest master at Ripon, he was visited by an angelic presence. One morning in December before the daylight had arrived, Cuthbert entered the guesthouse. Here already was a young man, white and still, though the whiteness was mainly frost and snow clinging to his clothes. Cuthbert bent down and rubbed the man's feet to bring warmth and feeling into them. Cuthbert asked the man to stay within the shelter of the guesthouse and said he would return to him with food after the morning prayers. He said, 'Refresh yourself, brother, and I will go and get you a warm loaf.' When Cuthbert returned the young man had gone, yet there were no tracks in the snow. Stranger still, there were three loaves smelling fresh and fragrant and looking very pure and white. He had intended to feed his visitor and it would seem the visitor had left food for Cuthbert. It was a mystery, but Cuthbert thought upon the words from Hebrews, 'Do not neglect to show hospitality to strangers, for thereby some have entertained angels unawares' (Hebrews 13.1). Cuthbert was convinced that this was an angelic visitation: once more he had seen an angel.

We may want to describe Cuthbert's angelic encounters differently, but in doing so we are in danger of closing our minds to a greater reality that is always about us. Let not the words he uses put us off the experience. Let me give you an example. When Cuthbert was 16, he was up in the hill country guarding sheep. This meant he had to keep alert, to be on the watch for any movement. In the night sky he said he saw angels descending then ascending and taking a holy soul to God. The next day he heard that Aidan had died. God had spoken to Cuthbert through this event, on 31 August 651. Cuthbert heeded the message and offered himself at the monastery at Melrose. In the year 1987 it was time to remember Cuthbert's own death, 1,300 years past. I came to Lindisfarne on 31 August because I felt drawn there. That night I went out with two strangers, as witnesses, to look at the night sky. Within seconds I saw a shooting star, then another and another. I had only seen one shooting star before and now I saw over a hundred. I was deeply moved. I later discovered that this band of meteors appears every year about this time, but I did not know it before. It was if the stars had a message, in the way that Archbishop Temple meant when he said, 'When I pray coincidences happen, when I do not pray they do not happen.' From then I felt an attraction to Lindisfarne and have now worked here since 1990. I would like to ask, 'Did I see stars or angels?' If you are students writing an essay on this I would award the most marks to those who answer 'Yes'! I have no doubt the stars had a message for me, and the Greek for 'messenger' is 'angel'. If we say to a messenger boy or girl, 'You are an angel', we are only stating a fact. We lose sight of angels if we restrict them to winged creatures dressed in white. When at college all tramps that visited were respected and called 'angels'. We tried to live by the words of the letter to the Hebrews, 'Do not neglect to show hospitality to strangers, for thereby some have entertained angels unawares' (Hebrews 13.1). Think over again the words of Francis Thompson:

> The angels keep their ancient places; –
> Turn but a stone, and start a wing!
> 'Tis ye, 'tis your estranged faces,
> That miss the many-splendoured thing.

The ability to see angels was not the only gift of sight that Cuthbert possessed: it would seem he could be aware of events over a distance and over a period of time. Cuthbert had travelled along Hadrian's Wall, almost to its western end to Carlisle. He was in the city to be with Queen Iurminburg, whose husband Egfrith had gone to war with the Picts. The people of Carlisle were proud of their history and Cuthbert was being shown the Roman walls and a fountain. Near to the fountain Cuthbert suddenly became greatly troubled in spirit. He groaned and looked to the ground, not wanting to face anyone. He leant on his staff and said, 'Oh, Oh, Oh.' At last when he looked up he said in a quiet voice, 'Perhaps even now the issue of the battle is decided.' The natural reaction came from a priest standing nearby: 'How do you know?' Cuthbert did not want to try and explain but replied, 'Do you not see how greatly changed and disturbed the weather is? What mortal being is able to enquire into the judgements of God?' On a more ordinary, practical level, Cuthbert immediately went to the Queen and advised her to return to the royal city straight away in case her life was in danger. He promised that after dedicating a church he would follow her to the palace.

With Cuthbert we see someone who has 'tuned the five stringed harp', the human senses, until they vibrate with what is going on around him. Too often when people say they are bored or that events around them are boring it is because they have become dull or allowed their life to be overcrowded. When people are insensitive to the mysteries and wonders of life, to the wonderful world or to people, they are not open to the glories of God, which are about them. People who close themselves up from wonder nearly always project God and his kingdom to another time and space and have little contact with him in the here and now. The more open we become to God, the more open we are to his creation: the more open we are to creation, the more open we become to God.

Cuthbert saw through the false divisions we make between heaven and earth, God and ourselves, other people and ourselves. Cuthbert was aware of a unity of creation that we have become insensitive to, though the modern world is learning once again that nothing stands alone, all things are in unity with other parts of God's Universe. Heaven is woven into our world, and is here and now. A world viewed with this insight gives us a vision of a world that is ablaze with the glory of God.

We need to reawaken our senses so that they will react to the depth and wonders of the world about us. Too often we have taken a closed-circuit attitude that will not let anything enter that is strange or challenging. We seek to be in control and in so doing limit our vision, our senses and our experiences. The world we live in has many levels and is multidimensional and yet we often opt for a narrow view with a tightly controlled environment.

I once went to a television studio for an interview where they aimed to be hard on me. I was questioned about whether I was in touch with reality. I had just travelled 30 miles over snow-covered moors and icy roads, skidding occasionally. I had stopped twice to help stranded motorists. I was fitting this interview in between an early morning service and visiting a group of people in hospital, at least one of whom was dying. For good measure the vicarage heating system was not working. They asked whether I was in touch with reality! In contrast, we were in a studio with no windows and air conditioning, and I had to take off two layers of clothing for comfort. The room was soundproofed and no one was allowed to enter without permission. They were shielded from all that was going on outside and here they lived day after day, and these were the people that wondered if I was in touch with reality. I pointed out that it depended what you thought reality was – and it was not always wrapped in safe or comprehensible bundles. Wherever we are there is a greater reality always waiting to be found and experienced. The reality I was talking about meant having an openness and a willingness to be worked on and changed by the elements of the world. We should find the world a great adventure, a challenge and spirit stretching. We must not retreat to safe systems or places or to cosy ideologies. We should let wonder and awe dispel any boredom and let ourselves come alive to the glory of God. To quote from Hamlet: 'There are more things in heaven and earth, Horatio, than are dreamt of in your philosophy.'

This vision we strive for is holistic in the sense that it discovers that all things are united and interwoven; nothing is separate or stands alone in our universe. If we were sensitive enough we would discover that if you pluck one string all tremble, whatever you do affects the world you live in. It is not true that what you do in private does not affect other people. There is a web of relationships that links all, from the tiniest particle to the whole universe. This mysterious web can be expressed by Celtic knot-work patterns with their ups and downs, their hidden and open designs. They are very complex but there is a pattern and there is no ending. These relationships are organic for they are living relationships; it is not about organizing but rather living alongside and with the other elements of the universe. This is a world to be treated with reverence and awe. Perhaps instead of seeking unity in our world we should rejoice that it is there already and seek to enrich our world by living that unity. Wholeness and holiness are the very fabric of our universe and of relationships between all things. For us, vision, if it is to have any meaning, always demands a response.

Not long after Cuthbert's vision of the defeat in battle he returned to Carlisle to ordain some priests and to clothe the Queen in her monastic habit, for Egfrith had died at Nectansmere as he predicted.

Whilst he was there, an old friend and hermit, Heribert, who had his hermitage on an island in Derwentwater, visited Cuthbert. For a good few years Heribert had travelled to see Cuthbert and to receive spiritual guidance. At the end of their conversation Cuthbert said, 'Remember, Heribert, to ask me for anything you need. Tell me about it now, for once we part we will not meet again on this earth.' Heribert was deeply distressed at this statement and fell at Cuthbert's knees with tears flowing. Heribert asked, 'I beseech you, dear Lord, not to leave me. Ask the merciful God, whom we have served together on this earth, that we may journey together to his kingdom in heaven.' Cuthbert was deeply moved by this sign of affection and loyalty. Both men remained in silence for quite a time. Cuthbert suddenly spoke and said, 'Rise dear friend. God has granted what you have asked.' No more was said about it by these two men, but the day that Cuthbert died Heribert at the other side of the country also died.

It is difficult for us in the twenty-first century to make sense of these stories because we have not the same world outlook. In many ways we are far better informed concerning our material world, but that is only half the picture and we have become blind to the greater world that is about us. I do believe it is important to have an informed and scientific outlook, but if that is all we have, we have become spiritually impoverished. We need to be able to see again not only with the eyes of science but with the eyes of our hearts. There are some wonderful words from the letter to the Ephesians:

having the eyes of your hearts enlightened, that you may
know what is the hope to which he has called you, what
are the riches of his glorious inheritance in the saints, and
what is the immeasurable greatness of his power in us
who believe.

(Ephesians 1.18–19)

To be without this vision of the world is to live
without being in touch with the reality of the wonder
and mystery that is all about us. Peter Berger in his
book *A Rumour of Angels* suggests that the recovery
of faith will come for many through the re-opening of
their eyes:

A rediscovery of the supernatural will be, above all, a
regaining of openness in our perception of reality. It will
not only be, as theologians influenced by existentialism
have greatly overemphasized, an overcoming of tragedy.
Perhaps more importantly it will be an overcoming of
triviality. In openness to the signals of the transcendence
the true proportions of our experience are rediscovered.
This is the comic relief of redemption; it makes it possible
for us to laugh and play with a new fullness.

(Berger, 1970, p. 119)

Often the eyes of our heart have not been allowed to
see deeply and further than is convenient: perhaps we
are afraid of being disturbed or disturbing others. If
we continue in this shallow view of life we cannot
hope to see beyond our narrow vision. There are many
worlds about us, and many ways of looking at the
world, but we often elect for a narrow view. We allow
the clouds to come down and shorten our vision. In
choosing one world-view, the other wonders and
expanses decrease. Reality becomes for us what it

seems, small and often dull and boring. We need to expand our sense of awe and wonder to look again upon the world with newness and openness. Then like the Celts of old we will see 'wonder upon wonder and every one of them true'. If you feel far from this, heed again the words of Teilhard de Chardin: 'You fail to get to the bottom of what goes on in your heart and your mind, and that is why the cosmic sense and faith in the world is still dormant in you' (Teilhard de Chardin, 1964, p. 40).

If we are so blind to the wonders of the world, how can we hope to behold the mystery and wonder of our God? It is by plunging into the depths and mystery of creation that we are able to discover the greater wonder of the Creator. It is through the world that God speaks to us, and it is through the created order that we gain our experience and our vision of God. We come to God through creation and our God comes to us through his created order. God and the world are not totally distinct from each other, though God is not dependent on the world: he is to be found within it and we are to discover it is in him.

The story of Cuthbert and the Eagle well illustrates these links with all things. Cuthbert had taken a boy into the hills to preach the gospel to the poor hill people. Cuthbert was teaching the boy and as they travelled together they recited psalms and parts of a Gospel. There were no books and they had learnt all this by heart: by heart and not mind only, for they were learnt in worship and not just in class. Because it was a fast day the two of them would not eat until three in the afternoon, the hour of Christ's death on the cross. They were offered hospitality at a farm where they had preached. Cuthbert refused to stay because there were more places to visit and there were greater hungers than food. At about three he asked the boy, 'Where do we find food here in the wilderness?' If I was the boy I would have kicked him. I find impractical Christians hard to bear. I cannot stand those who do not do anything and then say let us pray about it! It's even worse when their prayers are answered!! Cuthbert stretched out his arms in the shape of a cross and began to quietly pray. The boy watched. When you pray things do happen. Suddenly, flying high overhead was an eagle. This mighty bird dived towards them, into a stream and took out a salmon. Cuthbert told the boy to get the salmon. When the lad presented it Cuthbert gently told him, 'You have done wrong, for you must share the salmon with the eagle.' This done, the boy thought, 'salmon steaks'. Cuthbert spoke again, 'We cannot eat this. We must share it with a poor family.' Bede, the narrator of the story, tells us they did just this and simmered the salmon.

What a wonderful event, but more is going on than meets the eye. Was the eagle the Gospel of St John, the eagle gospel? Did the eagle provide the two with Ichthus, the fish, and which stands for Jesus, Christ, Son of God, Saviour? They received from John but they had to share with John their own experience. Then, once you have received the Christ, you must go and share, you cannot keep this to yourself. Note that they simmered the salmon: they took their time, they did not throw it at the people and leave, they slowly shared with them what they had received. Here is a story with a multitude of levels because life and the world has all these levels and more. As I asked earlier about angels in this chapter, I now ask about the eagle, 'Was it an eagle or was it St John's Gospel?' Again the knowing students will answer 'Yes'. For it is not one or the other; both are happening and it is our small vision that would separate them out. We need to learn to be vibrant people vibrating to the presence of our God and the wonders about us.

William Blake in 'A Memorable Fancy' has said, 'If the doors of the perception were cleansed everything would appear to man as it really is, infinite. For man has closed himself up, till he sees through narrow chinks of his cavern' (Bronowski, 1958, p. 101). So much of what we call spirituality is our perception of the world, others and ourselves. If we have become unable to see beyond the obvious and the sheer material we have become poor indeed. The danger for us all is 'one becomes what one sees'.

Teilhard de Chardin writes:

> Purity does not lie in separation from, but in a deeper penetration into the Universe . . . Bathe yourself in the ocean of matter: plunge into it where it is deepest and most violent; struggle in its currents and drink of its waters. For it cradled you long ago in your preconscious existence; and it is that ocean that will lift you up to God.
> (Teilhard de Chardin, 1970, p. 60)

In looking at the saints of the early church, we see that they were very much people of the world, but with a vision that led them on. These holy people were able to see beyond, to escape the trivial and to live in depth. The opportunity is still there for those who have the courage to take this road. Learn to be a pilgrim, to look beyond the obvious and to live life in the depths rather than be forever paddling in the shallows. Professor Alec King, in his book *Wordsworth and the Artist's Vision*, has some wonderful advice:

> What is necessary first for visionary powers is an undaunted appetite for liveliness – to be among the active elements of the world, and to love what they do to you, to love 'to work and be wrought upon'; to be alive to 'all that is enjoyed and all that is endured', to have the loneliness and courage to take in not only joy but dismay and fear and pain as modes of being without bolting for comfort or obscuring them by social chatter.
>
> (King, 1966, p. 20)

This challenging way to live is seen in his saints. We are called to reawaken, to retune our senses and know that in this wonderful world, 'In Him we live and move and have our being': and this is the reality of the situation we are in, it cannot be created by us, we can only deepen our awareness of it. Teilhard de Chardin says:

> God who made man that he might seek him – God whom we try to apprehend by the groping of our lives – that self-same God is as pervasive and perceptible as the atmosphere in which we are bathed. He encompasses us on every side, like the world itself. What prevents you then from enfolding him in your arms? Only one thing: your inability *to see him*.
>
> (Teilhard de Chardin, 1964, p. 46)

After Cuthbert had spent two strenuous years travelling as bishop of Lindisfarne, he returned to the island of Lindisfarne. He had poured himself out in caring for others and in the mission to which God had called him. He returned to the island knowing that he was terminally ill. He understood that the terminus is not the end of all but only one stage on a journey: the terminus is where you get off to go somewhere else; you do not stop at the terminus. Cuthbert needed to plan for his going over the edge of death and into life eternal.

Cuthbert sought permission from the brethren to go to a more remote island, Inner Farne, where he could concentrate on his future. On Inner Farne he dug a cell into the ground and raised up walls. It had no windows that could look out on the earth, only views of the heavens. Cuthbert had already set his sights on the future: as much as possible Cuthbert chose to walk and talk with God until the end came. When it did arrive, Cuthbert met it in worship and in communion and so he entered into glory. It was but a simple step into the kingdom and into the nearer presence of God. Cuthbert could have well rejoiced in his future as Augustine of Hippo rejoiced, saying:

> All shall be Amen and Alleluia.
> We shall rest and we shall see,
> We shall see and we shall know,
> We shall know and we shall love,
> We shall love and we shall praise,
> Behold our end, which is no end.
>
> (Quoted in Tutu, 1995, p. 33)

Cuthbert was used to looking forward and to eternity. It mattered not if his time on earth was long or short, what mattered was that he walked the edge of life with a deepening vision of the ever-present God. Such a vision is life transforming and gives us a much greater freedom to live our daily lives. Those who fear death are often afraid to live life to the full, afraid to become pilgrims and adventurers for God. Teilhard de Chardin faced his own death in the way Cuthbert did and wrote,

> That I may recognize you Under the species of each alien and hostile force that seems bent upon destroying or uprooting me ... It is you painfully parting my fibres in order to penetrate the very marrow of my substance and bear me away within yourself ... It is not enough that I should die communicating ... teach me that death is a communion.
>
> (Teilhard de Chardin, 1964, p. 90)

When we finally lose our grip on life and fall over the edge, we find we are grasped and held by the living God.

Exercises

1   Be still in the presence of God and say slowly:

> Lord, open my eyes
> To the wonder of the world
> And your presence within it.
> Lord open my ears
> To the calls of creation
> And to your voice quiet and near.
> Lord open my heart
> To the love of others
> And to your love close and real.
> Lord open each sense and make aware
> Of the wonder and beauty always there.

2 Seek to discover God through the wonders of all of creation. Everything that exists is full of mystery and has the potential to reveal the Divine. Nothing is profane for all is in God. If we are to learn from the saints, we must discover that God is to be met in the ordinary things of the world. In the same way we can find our God in the mystery of our own life. Think upon these words of St Columbanus: 'Understand the creation, if you wish to know the Creator: if you will not know the former either, be silent concerning the Creator, but believe in the Creator.'

3 Think upon these words:

> A person with a vision and no action is a dreamer.
> A person with much action and no vision is a drudge.
> A person with vision and action is a prophet.

4 Pray:

> Be thou my vision, O Lord of my heart,
> Be all else but naught to me, save that thou art:
> Be thou my best thought in the day and the night,
> Both waking and sleeping thy presence my light.

5 Affirm regularly:

> All shall be Amen and Alleluia.
> We shall rest and we shall see,
> We shall see and we shall know,
> We shall know and we shall love,
> We shall love and we shall praise,
> Behold our end, which is no end.

Walking the Edges

Within the heart of our world God is present, though often hidden: at the same time our world is within the heart of God. If our heart has not met his heart it is because we have not looked deep enough, we have stayed away from the edge in fear of the depths that are about us. Sadly, we fill ourselves with things that cannot either last or satisfy when the great God is seeking to fill us with his goodness and his very self. Augustine of Hippo expresses this well in the *Soliloquies* I,3a:

> God of our Blessedness,
> The source, beginning and creator of joy
> And of all that is joyful;
> God of goodness and beauty
> Who is in all that is good and beautiful;
> God our discernible Light,
> Who can be discerned in all that shines with that
>   light;
> God whose kingdom is the whole universe
> That our senses cannot perceive;
> God whose kingdom lays down laws for the
>   kingdoms of this world;
> God from whom to stray is to fall,

And to who to turn to is to rise up,
In whom to remain is to rest on a firm foundation.
To leave you is to die,
To return to you is to come back to life,
To dwell in you is to live.

(Boldoni, 1987, p. 87)

Every time we close our eyes to beauty, wonder or mystery we allow ourselves to die. Each time we open our lives to the presence of God we live and are renewed. Time and again God calls us out of death and into life. We need to find times of solitude and silence that we may heed his call. The Celtic monks were told to 'live near a city but not in it'; this may not be practical for us but we can make our own space and time to be more aware of our God. The wonderful thing is that, whenever we turn, God is waiting to meet us and accept us; this is the main teaching of the parable of the Prodigal Son (Luke 15.11–31; see especially verse 20). St Augustine of Hippo has said, 'No one ever calls upon Him without first being called by Him.' We see this time and again in the Scriptures. We are told that by faith Abraham went out not knowing where he was going (Hebrews 11.8). When Jacob left home God called him at Bethel; it was God calling him out. Jacob's response to the call of God was to awake out of sleep and say ' "Surely the LORD is in this place; and I did not know it." And he was afraid, and said, "How awesome is this place! This is none other than the house of God, and this is the gate of heaven" ' (Genesis 28.16–17).

In the silence and solitude of the desert, God calls Moses through the burning bush. Again God calls before he is called upon. Moses is called into the deep, out of the safety and security of Pharaoh's court to go into the desert. Too often we want the riches of the Promised Land, but we are unwilling to cross the desert. The writer to the Hebrews says of Moses that he chose 'rather to share ill-treatment with the people of God than to enjoy the fleeting pleasures of sin. He considered abuse for the sake of Christ greater wealth than the treasures of Egypt. For he looked to the reward' (Hebrews 11.25–6). God told Moses that he would not be alone and that he was to tell the people to move out of Egypt and into the danger of the desert. They were to go out in faith, believing that God would provide. Moses was to tell the people when they hesitated to go forward, to set their sights on the horizon.

An old fisherman gave me some advice against seasickness: 'Never look at the waves threatening you with their rise and fall; do not look at the deck of the ship as it heaves up and down; keep your eyes on the horizon and you will come through.' I am not sure this works all the time but I have learnt to fix my eyes on the horizon. Like the people of Israel entering the desert, I have learnt to move forward in hope. God's call comes to all of us to move forward; we may not know the outcome of various events in our lives but we are all promised an abiding presence and a glorious future. There is a beautiful prayer that is attributed to St Brendan when he is being challenged to move forward:

> Shall I abandon, O king of the Mysteries, the soft
>   comforts of home?
> Shall I turn my back on my native land, and my
>   face towards the sea?

Shall I put myself wholly at the mercy of God,
    without silver, without horse, without fame, and
    honour?
Shall I throw myself wholly on the King of kings,
    without sword and shield,
    without food and drink, without a bed to lie on?
Shall I say farewell to my beautiful land, placing
    myself under Christ's yoke?
Shall I pour out my heart to him, confessing my
    manifold sins,
    and begging forgiveness, tears streaming down
    my cheeks?

Shall I leave the prints of my knees on the sandy
    beach,
    a record of my final prayer in my native land?
Shall I then suffer every kind of wound the sea
    can then inflict?

Shall I take my tiny coracle across the wide,
    sparkling ocean?
O King of Glorious Heaven, shall I go of my own
    choice upon the sea?
O Christ will you help me on the wild waves?
                    (Van de Weyer, 1990, p. 30)

Obviously every question knows that the answer is
'Yes.' When God calls too often the human stalls.
Every day we are given the opportunity to extend our
lives, to reach out and be touched by God: every day
God waits for us to turn to him. We need to be willing
to walk the edges and to say 'Yes' to God.

Dag Hammarskjöld in *Markings* asks a similar
question to that of Brendan and expects the same sort
of answer:

I am being driven forward
Into an unknown land,
The pass grows steeper,
The air colder and sharper.
A wind from my unknown goal
Stirs the strings of expectation.
Still the question:
Shall I ever get there?
There where life resounds
A clear white note.
In the silence.

(Hammarskjöld, 1964, p. 31)

When such a question arises, we are called to venture. Brendan went towards what he thought was the very edge of the world. If we fail to reach out we are killing the life that is in us. Too often fear holds us back; we show a lack of trust, a lack of faith. It is true there will be deserts or oceans to cross, our own innermost darkness to penetrate, but we are not alone: our God is with us. God not only calls us, he empowers us. We often look for the sheltering wings of God: we look for God's safety and comfort, rather than listen to his call to 'launch out into the deep'. Yet faith is often revealed when we adventure and risk for God. Dag Hammarskjöld (p. 169) says, 'Once I answered Yes to Someone – or Some thing. And from that hour I was certain that existence is meaningful, that therefore, my life, in self-surrender has a goal.'

When the Israelites were struggling and Moses was troubled, God reminded them: 'You have seen what I did to the Egyptians, and how I bore you on eagles' wings and brought you to myself' (Exodus 19.4). It is not so much the sheltering wings we need but the wings of the eagle! We need the courage to do things as much as we need the protection from dangers: we need the courage to step out in faith.

It was thought that when the time came for a young eaglet to fly it was encouraged to leave the nest by the call of the parent. The mighty bird would fly past and call. If this failed, the nestlings were made uncomfortable by having their food supply greatly reduced: if they did not fly they would die. The security of the ledge was not to be a way of life: the bird must be encouraged to jump out into the new world before it. The parent would fly past calling and urging the young to come to the edge. This must have been a strange moment for a bird, which had never tested its wings, as new abilities and talents were being called for. At last an eaglet would leap out and fly. Suddenly a young bird caught in a down draught would spiral toward the earth, unable to cope on its own. The parent bird, eagle-eyed, would then swoop down to beneath the bird and bear it up, raising it skyward until it could take off again. The eaglet would be encouraged to try again and again until it could fly unaided and be at home in the air. The French poet Guillaume Apollinaire captured this adventure when he wrote:

> Come to the edge,
> He said. They said,
> We are afraid.
> Come to the edge
> He said. They came
> He pushed them, and
>   they flew.

(Quoted in O'Malley, 1997, p. 146)

The saints we have looked at in this book call us to walk the edges, to adventure and risk for the love of God, to discover a deep and more profound world than the small, artificially safe world we make for ourselves. Come and stand where the wind blows freely, come and be silent before your God and hear his calling to you. God is not a theory to be studied. He is the 'God with whom we have to do': God wants each of us to enjoy a personal relationship with him. God is not a great problem for us to seek to solve: he is a great mystery to be enjoyed. If our minds are too small to grasp this, we can discover our hearts are big enough to accept it. Heed quietly these words:

> You have called me by name,
> In the night, across the years;
> You have called my name,
> In my laughter and my tears.
> The words are never quite the same,
> Seeking out my dulled ears;
> Wanting me to rise and wake,
> To cast away my doubts and fears.
> Your love is there for me to take;
> More than this, I should know,
> When the day is turned to night,
> You are there, wherever I go,
> My love, calling me to light.
> Calling me at every breath,
> Calling me to rise from death.

So come, walk the edges and enjoy the glorious freedom of the children of God. God give you grace to walk the way of his saints in joy, peace and love: to discover the beauty of his holiness and to enjoy his Presence.

Exercises

1 Read the Call of the Fishermen (Luke 5.1–11). Picture the event. See the fishermen as they look to their nets. They are tired and disappointed men: no catch of fish means no income: empty nets can mean an empty stomach. Into the emptiness Jesus enters and sits in their boat. He asks a small act of friendship in borrowing their boat. Now he asks them to thrust out a little from the land. They were ready to sleep, but Jesus asks of them this small action. From the boat he talks to the crowds and to them. Then he asks them to launch out into the deep. Immediately there is an objection, but at the same time they are willing to do what he asks, even to the letting down of their nets. When we obey it is amazing what great things happen. Their nets were full of fish to the point of breaking. A wonderful catch, but a more wonderful catch had taken place: Jesus had caught the disciples and he says 'Follow me.'

Ponder, think over how gentle was the call and how gradual.

> A borrowed boat.
> 'Thrust out a little.'
> 'Launch out into the deep.'
> 'Let down your net.'
> 'Follow me.'

At any stage the disciples could have refused. Too often we fail to enter the deep because we are not even willing to meet small requests that disturb our routine, nor are we willing to thrust out a little from our present situation. It is when we take the first steps in small things that we can then be approached by the greater call, which says to us 'Follow me.' Are you really making enough effort to move out a little? Promise that you will give heed each day to the Presence of God and to the mysteries that are about you.

Pray slowly and carefully:

Lord, open my eyes to your presence
In the world that is about me.
Lord, open my ears to your call
Make me attentive of you.
Open my heart to your love
As revealed in those who love me.

2 Think over these words:

Only those who walk the paths know more than
the maps:
Only those who enjoy the Presence can truly talk
of God.

3 Say slowly or sing:

Guide me, O Thou great Redeemer,
Pilgrim through this barren land;
I am weak but Thou art mighty,
Hold me with Thy powerful hand;
Bread of Heaven,
Feed me now and evermore.

Open now the crystal fountain,
Whence the healing streams do flow:
Let the fiery cloudy pillar
Lead me all my journey through;
Strong Deliverer,
Be Thou still my Strength and Shield.

When I tread the verge of Jordan,
Bid my anxious fears subside:
Death of death, and hell's destruction,
Land me safe on Canaan's side;
Songs of praises,
I will ever give to Thee. Amen.

(William Williams, 1717–91)

4 Seek to know the depth of these words of George
  Fox (1624–1691): 'Walk cheerfully over the world,
  answering that of God in everyone.'

References and Further Reading

Adam, David, 2001, *A Celtic Psaltery*, SPCK.

Adam, David, 1991, *Border Lands: The Best of David Adam*, SPCK.

Adam, David, 2003, *Fire of the North: The Life of St Cuthbert*, SPCK.

Adam, David, 1997, *Flame in My Heart: St Aidan for Today*, Triangle.

Adam, David, 1987, *The Cry of the Deer: Meditations on the Hymn of St Patrick*, Triangle.

Adam, David, 1985, *The Edge of Glory: Prayers in the Celtic Tradition*, SPCK.

Bede, trans. Leo Sherley-Price, 1955, *A History of the English Church and People*, Penguin.

Berger, Peter, 1970, *A Rumour of Angels*, Penguin Press.

Bloom, Anthony, 1966, *Living Prayer*, Darton, Longman & Todd.

Boldoni, Valeria (compiler), 1987, *Praying with St Augustine*, Triangle.

Bonhoeffer, Dietrich, 1952, *Life Together*, Harper & Row.

Bronowski, J. (ed.), 1958, *William Blake*, Penguin.

Carmichael, Alexander, 1983 (Vol. 1), 1976 (Vol. 2), *Carmina Gadelica*, Scottish Academic Press.

Colgrave, Bertram, 1985, *Two Lives of St Cuthbert*, Cambridge University Press.

De Caussade, trans. A. Thorold, 1933, *Self-Abandonment to Divine Providence*, Burns, Oates & Washbourne.

De La Mare, Walter, 1928, *Come Hither: A Collection of Rhymes and Poems*, Constable.

Donaldson, Christopher, 1980, *Martin of Tours*, Routledge & Kegan Paul.

Every, George *et al.* (eds), 1984, *Seasons of the Spirit*, Triangle.

Gardner, W. H. (ed.), 1953, *Gerard Manley Hopkins*, Penguin.

Hammarskjöld, Dag, 1964, *Markings*, Faber and Faber.

Harries, Richard, 1983, *Praying Round the Clock*, Mowbray.

Julian of Norwich, 1980, *Enfolded in Love*, Darton, Longman & Todd.

King, Alec, 1966, *Wordsworth and the Artist's Vision*, Athlone Press.

Kinsella, Thomas (trans.), 1970, *The Tain*, Oxford University Press.

Leatham, Diana, 1948, *They Built on Rock*, Celtic Art Society.

Meyer, Kuno (trans.), 1928, *Selections from Ancient Irish Poetry*, Constable.

O'Donoghue, Noel Dermot, 1987, *Aristocracy of Soul: Patrick of Ireland*, Darton, Longman & Todd.

O'Malley, Brendan, 1997, *God at Every Gate*, Canterbury Press.

Rees, Elizabeth, 2000, *Celtic Saints, Passionate Wanderers*, Thames & Hudson.

Severus, trans. Alexander Roberts, 1894, *Life of Martin*, Works of Sulpitius Severus, Vol. 11, James Parker.

Stancliffe, Clare and Eric, 1995, *Oswald, Northumbrian King and European Saint*, Paul Watkins.

Teilhard de Chardin, Pierre, 1970, *Hymn of the Universe*, Fontana.

Teilhard de Chardin, Pierre, 1964, *Le Milieu Divin*, Fontana.

Tutu, Desmond, 1995, *An African Prayer Book*, Hodder & Stoughton.

Two Lives of Celtic Saints, The Lives of Ninian and Kentigern, 1989, Lanerch Enterprises.

Van de Weyer, Robert, 1990, *Celtic Fire*, Darton, Longman & Todd.

Whiteside, Lesley, 1997, *In Search of St Columba*, Columba Press.

Whiteside, Lesley, 1996, *The Spirituality of St Patrick*, Columba Press.

Wright, Charles H. H., 1889, *The Writings of Patrick: The Apostle of Ireland*, Religious Tract Society.

Acknowledgements

The author and publisher gratefully acknowledge permission to reproduce copyright material. Every effort has been made to trace and acknowledge copyright holders. We apologize for any errors or omissions that may remain, and would ask those concerned to contact the publisher, who will ensure that full acknowledgements are made in a subsequent edition of this book.

Unless otherwise marked, Scripture quotations are from the New Revised Standard Version of the Bible, copyright © 1989 by the Division of Christian Education of the National Council of the Churches of Christ in the USA. Used by permission. All rights reserved.

Extracts from the Authorized Version of the Bible (The King James Bible), the rights in which are vested in the Crown, are reproduced by permission of the Crown's Patentee, Cambridge University Press.

Ninian's Catechism, on p. 67, and the prayer attributed to St Brendan, on pp. 139–40, are taken from *Celtic Fire* by Robert van de Weyer, published and copyright 1990 by Darton, Longman & Todd Ltd, and used by permission of the publishers.